STUDIES IN ENGLISH LITERATURE

Volume LXIV

THE LOVE PLAY
OF
ANTONY AND CLEOPATRA

A Critical Study of Shakespeare's Play

by

PHILIP J. TRACI

1970
MOUTON
THE HAGUE · PARIS

© Copyright 1970 in The Netherlands.
Mouton & Co. N.V., Publishers, The Hague.

*No part of this book may be translated or reproduced in any form,
by print, photoprint, microfilm, or any other means, without written
permission from the publishers.*

LIBRARY OF CONGRESS CATALOG CARD NUMBER: 77-106458

Printed in The Netherlands by Mouton & Co., Printers, The Hague.

For Betty Lou

ACKNOWLEDGMENTS

Professor John L. Lievsay, for directing the dissertation from which this work arises.

Professors Sylvan Barnet, Joseph A. Bryant, Jr., Alfred Harbage, Dorothy C. Hockey, Harold Jenkins, and Kenneth O. Myrick, from whom I have learned of Shakespeare's plays (whether as student or assistant) in the classroom.

Mr. John Cunningham, for sharing with me his knowledge of critical theory.

The library staffs of Duke, Harvard, and Tufts Universities.

The Danforth Foundation, for the grant which allowed me to complete the dissertation upon which this work is based.

Professor Allan H. Gilbert, who has long been my Virgil, for his continual encouragement.

P. J. T.

CONTENTS

I

LOVE AND LIMITATIONS: THE PLAY AND ITS CRITICS

"I'll set a bourn how far to be belov'd", [1] cries Cleopatra, and the
critics have complied by limiting their love for her play with
Antony. Caution invades even Coleridge's famous praise of the
play as "of all perhaps of Shakespeare's plays the most wonderful".[2] While the intensity of the critics' involvement may be
glimpsed in their adjectives, so may a lack of intellectual com-
mitment: "the most magnificent of Shakespeare's plays",[3] "very
noble",[4] and "the most spacious of the plays".[5] And there is that
inevitable "perhaps". Even G. Wilson Knight, never one to spare
an unqualified superlative, dubs *Antony and Cleopatra*, "probably
the subtlest and greatest play in Shakespeare, or, at least para-
goned only by *The Tempest*".[6] From beneath the exuberance of

[1] William Shakespeare, *Antony and Cleopatra*, ed. M. R. Ridley (London, Methuen, 1954), I, i, 16. All quotations from *Antony and Cleopatra*
in this work are from this New Arden Edition. All other Shakespearean
quotations are from his *Complete Plays and Poems* edited by William
Allan Neilson and Charles Jarvis Hill (New York, The Riverside Press,
1942). This new Cambridge Edition adheres to the standard lineation of
The Globe Edition.

[2] Samuel Taylor Coleridge, *Shakespearean Criticism*, ed. Thomas Middleton Raysor (Cambridge, Massachusetts, Harvard University Press,
1930), I, 86.

[3] G. B. Harrison, *Shakespeare's Tragedies* (London, Routledge and Kegan
Paul, 1951), p. 203.

[4] William Hazlitt, *Characters of Shakespear's Plays* (London, C. H.
Reynell, 1817), p. 95.

[5] Harley Granville-Barker, *Prefaces to Shakespeare*, second series (London, Sidgwick and Jackson, 1930), p. 111.

[6] G. Wilson Knight, *The Imperial Theme. Further Interpretations of
Shakespeare's Tragedies Including the Roman Plays* (London, Oxford University Press, 1931), p. 199.

the adjectives, moreover, there emerges the critic's apology for having himself become a slave to Passion. While Reason governs his judgment of the rest of the canon, it has no power here. *Antony and Cleopatra* is different. Its appeal is emotional, he says, and stems from its lyrical power, a power somehow separated from its content. Coleridge stands in awe at the *Feliciter audax* of its style,[7] and Chambers marvels at Shakespeare's "height of poetic expression".[8] But a reasonable awareness of its lack of drama or profundity characteristically accompanies the praise of its style. Thus Claudel thought the poetry superb, but the play itself not a very good one.[9] Often these limitations are forcefully implied: "virtuosic", "dazzlingly original",[10] or "brilliant *tour de force*", "perhaps Shakespeare's high-water-mark of sheer technical brilliance".[11]

This dazzle obscures the flaws of the play, some critics contend; others, that it lacks "the art that conceals art".[12] So overpowering is this brilliance in one critic's view that "*Antony and Cleopatra* is liable to exaltation at the expense of its tragic implications . . .".[13] Another acknowledges that while it is "a great achievement in drama and in poetry" and "authentically Shakespeare too", it is the product of "a Shakespeare . . . whose inward eye is dimming".[14] Although "his hand has lost none of its cunning", he continues, and "his imagination ranges widely as ever over space and time", it "dwells more on surfaces and no longer

---

[7]   Coleridge, I, 86.

[8]   E. K. Chambers, *William Shakespeare. A Study of Facts and Problems* (Oxford, Clarendon Press, 1930), I, 86.

[9]   Paul Claudel, cited in Robert Speaight, *Nature in Shakespearian Tragedy* (New York, Crowell-Collier, 1962), p. 131.

[10]   Lord David Cecil, "*Antony and Cleopatra*", The Fourth W. P. Ker Memorial Lecture delivered in the University of Glasgow, 4 May 1943 (Glasgow, Jackson, Son and Company, 1944), p. 11.

[11]   Ridley (New Arden), p. 1.

[12]   Longinus, "On Literary Excellence", trans. Allan H. Gilbert in *Literary Criticism Plato to Dryden* (New York, American Book Company, 1940), pp. 170-171.

[13]   W. B. C. Watkins, *Shakespeare and Spenser* (Cambridge, Massachusetts, Walker-de Berry, 1961), p. 31.

[14]   H. B. Charlton, *Shakespearian Tragedy* (Cambridge, University Press, 1961), p. 15.

thrusts to the utter depths". The play, in his critical judgment, is "more remarkable for the artistry than for the genius of the artist displayed".[15] Granville-Barker asserts that "we have a play of action, then, not of spiritual insight".[16] G. B. Harrison agrees that *Antony and Cleopatra* is "not a deep tragedy", and adds, "indeed Shakespeare never intended it to be".[17] Traversi sees the whole problem of the play as involved with this "interpretation of the author's true intention", for

sooner or later, indeed the critic finds himself faced by two interpretations of Shakespeare's intention in this play, each of them strongly defended and each of them arguing from elements demonstrably present in the text, whose only disadvantage is that they appear to be mutually exclusive. Is *Antony and Cleopatra*, to put the matter in other terms, a tragedy of lyrical inspiration, justifying love by presenting it as triumphant over death, or is it rather a remorseless exposure of human frailties, a presentation of spiritual possibilities dissipated through a senseless surrender to passion?[18]

Whatever the answer, Traversi proposes that we search for it in the Intentional Fallacy.

Many other critics, however, attribute the ambiguity of the play more to its "loose" structure than to its author's lack of clear intention. The possibility of conscious structural ambiguity [19] is ignored. H. B. Charlton points to the "wide diversity between the ultra-romantic structure of *Antony and Cleopatra* and the classical formality of *Coriolanus*".[20] Although the reasons may vary, the judgment that the play is "the most faultily constructed of all the tragedies" [21] has rarely been questioned.

More devastating are those critics who, like Lord David Cecil, assert that the play "is not dramatic at all, in the sense that *Othello* is dramatic". "Nor", he adds, "is *Antony and Cleopatra*

---

[15] *Ibid.*
[16] Granville-Barker, *Prefaces to Shakespeare*, p. 111.
[17] Harrison, *Shakespeare's Tragedies*, p. 226.
[18] D. A. Traversi, *An Approach to Shakespeare* (New York, Doubleday and Company, 1956), p. 235.
[19] See discussion of "question structure", Chapter V.
[20] Charlton, p. 15.
[21] A. C. Bradley, *Shakespearean Tragedy. Lectures on "Hamlet", "Othello", "King Lear", "Macbeth"* (London, Macmillan, 1905), p. 260.

tragic, as *King Lear* is tragic".[22] Bradley offers support in his contention that the play lacks action as well as spiritual insight: "People converse, discuss, accuse one another, excuse themselves, mock, describe, drink together, arrange a marriage, meet and part; but they do not kill, do not even tremble and weep." [23] Despite the verbs Bradley is forced to use in his description of the first three acts of the play alone, he sees little he would call action. "Almost nothing", he notes. With Ridley as with Bradley, we learn more of his definition of drama than of the play. "The story of Antony's relation to Cleopatra", he says, "is not essentially dramatic at all; there is no progress, merely an oscillation. Under various influences – loyalty to Octavia, loyalty to Rome, and, by far the strongest, love of being a great fighting general and leading his adoring troops – Antony swings like a compass needle, but comes to rest always pointing to the inevitable north." [24] Although Ridley's comment is undoubtedly without pun, by it we should be led to believe that North's progressive narrative is more dramatic than Shakespeare's oscillating play. Even after admitting that "it would be inept to consider *Antony and Cleopatra* simply as a poem", Norman Holmes Pearson lends his support to the idea that it is more poem than play. Here, he observes, "words become supreme ... almost at the expense of action, [and] we approach the realm of the closet drama rather than the theatre". We are "very close", he cautions, "to that line which divides poetic drama from a dramatic poem", a fact he charges to "the intensely, almost metaphysically contrived verbal texture of *Antony and Cleopatra*".[25] Lord Devid Cecil aptly describes the prevailing critical attitude toward the play:

[22] Lord David Cecil, pp. 8-9. Cf. Hardin Craig, *An Interpretation of Shakespeare* (New York, The Dryden Press, 1948), p. 268: "Nowhere does Shakespeare grasp more fully the real nature of tragedy than in the story of Antony ...".
[23] A. C. Bradley, *Oxford Lectures on Poetry* (London, Macmillan, 1934), p. 284.
[24] Ridley (New Arden), p. ix.
[25] Norman Holmes Pearson, *"Antony and Cleopatra"* in *Shakespeare: Of An Age and For All Time*, The Yale Shakespeare Festival Lectures, ed. Charles Tyler Prouty (New Haven, Connecticut, The Shoe String Press, 1954), p. 128.

In spite of all the praise that has been lavished on it, its position among Shakespeare's works has remained ambiguous . . . . Their authors all speak of it as one of Shakespeare's greatest performances: they all agree that it contains some of his most magnificent work. But, in the midst of their paeans of praise, they suddenly let fall a sentence which shows their feelings about it are divided, that they do not quite know what to make of it.[26]

This I-love-you-but-I-don't-understand-you sounds in Coleridge's grudging admission that "the highest praise or rather form of praise, of this play, which I can offer in my own mind, is the doubt which its perusal always occasions in me, whether it is not in all exhibitions of a giant power in its strength and vigor of maturity, a formidable rival of *Macbeth, Lear, Othello,* and *Hamlet*".[27] Few other critics have felt even doubt. "Of late", Allardyce Nicoll observes of these few, "various endeavors have been made to elevate *Antony and Cleopatra* to a position equal with that of the four great tragedies, and we have been asked to see in it the very finest expression of Shakespeare's genius." "Despite the wonder" that he says arises from our awareness that "a mature Shakespeare, absolute master of his art, rules majestically over the dialogue", the play has "rarely had for the reader or spectator the same power as that possessed by any of the four great tragedies".[28] Most critics, however, even of late, would, like Hazlitt, assign the play a position "though not in the first class of Shakespeare's productions", yet "next to them".[29] A. C. Bradley protests, perhaps too much, that

to regard this tragedy as a rival of the famous four, whether on the stage or in the study, is surely an error. The world certainly has not so regarded it; and, though the world's reasons for its verdicts on works of art may be worth little, its mere verdict is worth much. Here, it seems to me, that verdict must be accepted. One may notice that, in calling *Antony and Cleopatra* wonderful or astonishing, we appear to be thinking first of the artist and his activity, while in the

---

[26] Lord David Cecil, p. 7.
[27] Coleridge, I, 86.
[28] Allardyce Nicoll, *Shakespeare: An Introduction* (New York, Oxford University Press, 1952), p. 151.
[29] Hazlitt, p. 95.

case of the four famous tragedies it is the product of this activity, the thing presented that first engrosses us.[30]

Still another explanation offered for "what keeps it from being another *Macbeth* is a certain retreat from universalization". Dryden, continues Hazelton Spencer, is able to mold "the old clay" of Cleopatra into "Woman in Love", while Shakespeare retains her as "that identical dusky Egyptian (as he supposed her to be), and none other".[31] Theodore Spencer finds his reason for the play's falling short of the four great tragedies in a contrast with *Lear*, for "as large as the world of *Antony and Cleopatra* may be", he explains, "it is a very different world from that of *Lear*. It may be immensely imposing, it may be rich, spacious and magnificent – but it is a world of the senses; it is physical. Lear's world is metaphysical; it is the world of the soul." [32] The contradiction by which one critic condemns the play for its metaphysical, non-dramatic texture and another derides its purely physical focus characterizes the analyses of the play. That the physical and metaphysical may be intrinsically linked is a possibility eloquently raised in the play itself. The physical emphasis disturbs Dryden as well, who steers "the middle course" in *All for Love*, for " 'tis true, some actions, tho' natural, are not fit to be represented; and broad obscenities in words ought in good manners to be avoided: expressions therefore are a modest clothing of our thoughts, as breeches and petticoats are of our bodies".[33] The implications of Dryden's statement are, of course, that some of the actions of Shakespeare's Antony and Cleopatra, though natural, are not fit to be represented in a play that, unlike his,

---

[30] Bradley, *Oxford Lectures on Poetry*, p. 280.

[31] Hazelton Spencer, *The Art and Life of William Shakespeare* (New York, Harcourt, Brace and Company, 1940), p. 341. One can only wonder at Hazelton Spencer's contention that Shakespeare retains Cleopatra as "that dusky Egyptian ... and none other".

[32] Theodore Spencer, *Shakespeare and the Nature of Man* (New York, Macmillan, 1961), p. 169.

[33] John Dryden, Preface to "All for Love or The World Well Lost: A Tragedy Written in Imitation of Shakespere's Style" in *Selected Dramas*, ed. George R. Noyes (New York, Scott, Foresman and Company, 1910), p. 230.

presents "no middle flight".[34] The limitations of Shaw's love for
the play may be readily seen in the rhetorical question that forms
the title of his preface to *Caesar and Cleopatra*: "Better than
Shakespeare?" [35] *Antony and Cleopatra*, then, "one of the most
neglected works in the canon",[36] has also been "treated the least
kindly of Shakespeare's great tragedies".[37]

The charge of neglect of the text must extend to evasive criticism as well as to the generalized emotional reactions we have
already noted. Indeed infinite variety characterizes the techniques
by which the critics have ingeniously avoided the work itself.
Occasionally the criticism reveals only the period in which it was
written or the personality of its author. Many late nineteenth-
century German critics, for example, focus on North's translation of Plutarch rather than on the significance of Shakespeare's
adherence to or divergence from his primary source. The same
emphasis is true of comparisons and contrasts with Dryden's
"tragedy written in imitation of Shakespeare's style".[38] If less
common, studies of Horace's influence on the play,[39] or
that of the Book of Revelation,[40] or of Cleopatra as Venus,[41]

[34]   John Milton, *Paradise Lost*, ed. Merritt Y. Hughes (New York, The
Odyssey Press, 1935), I, 14.
[35]   George Bernard Shaw, "Three Plays for Puritans", in *Collected Plays*
(New York, Herbert S. Stone and Company, 1901), p. xxviii.
[36]   Dolora G. Cunningham, "The Characterization of Shakespeare's Cleopatra", *Shakespeare Quarterly*, VI (1955), 9.
[37]   S. L. Bethell, *Shakespeare and the Popular Dramatic Tradition* (New
York, Staples Press, 1944), p. 116.
[38]   Dryden, see footnote 33, p. 16 above. Cf. F. R. Leavis, "*Antony and
Cleopatra* and *All for Love*: A Critical Exercise", *Scrutiny*, V (1936-37),
158: "Dryden and Shakespeare seem to be doing things so different in
kind as to make a serious and sustained comparison obviously impossible . . .".
[39]   See Perry D. Westbrook, for example, "Horace's Influence on Shakespeare's *Antony and Cleopatra*", *PMLA*, LXII (June, 1947), 392-398.
[40]   See, for example, Ethel Seaton, "*Antony and Cleopatra* and the Book
of Revelation", *Review of English Studies*, XXII (July, 1946), 219-224.
[41]   See, for example, Mara Ruta Maizitis, "A Reading of *Troilus* and The
Roman Plays" (Unpublished Ph.D. dissertation: Yale University, 1959),
p. 142: "Yet once Cleopatra is thus established as Venus (and it takes the
unexpected reaction of Enobarbus to do this), it is easy to see her capturing
the Roman God of War ('those his goodly eyes,/ That o'er the files and
musters of the war/ Have glow'd like plated Mars,' I, i, 2-4), and turning

Isis,[42] Dido, or Omphale [43] have proven equally evasive. Neither has Elizabethan background remained in its proper place. Too often the play has been its foil. Analyses such as Daniel Stempel's are too frequent:

Here our knowledge of Elizabethan mores can come to our aid. ...
Woman was a creature of weak reason and strong passions, carnal in nature and governed by lust. She could be trusted only when guided by the wisdom of her natural superior, man. ... She is not so much a tragic slave of passion in herself as a symbol of Antony's slavery to desire. She is the tempter and the temptation; she destroys the balance of Antony's nature by arousing his physical desire to the point where it defeats his reason. ... The misogyny of Octavius is founded on right reason. His one general statement on the nature of woman [III, xii, 29-31] echoes the sentiments of Shakespeare's contemporaries. ...
Lust and physical gratification are constant themes. This is in keeping with the general premise, familiar to all in Shakespeare's time, that eroticism is the primary motivation of women. There are also, however, more specific and less obvious trends of imagery which stem directly from Renaissance misogyny. These images are all associated with Cleopatra and fall into three classes: references to magic and witchcraft, to poisons, and to serpents. It is clear that these are actually a single group united by the common theme of witchcraft in its broadest (and worst) connotations.[44]

Here the background takes the foreground. Never is the tone of a specific passage considered. Never is dramatic sympathy mentioned.[45] Surely no sensitive spectator ever agrees exclusively with Octavius' "right reason". The fact that Antony's faults are pre-

---

him into a Mars in chains, for the whole Roman world to watch, comment on, and ultimately envy. Venus, however, has other guises: and Cleopatra uttering her lament over the body of her lover reminds us, rather, of Venus bending over the wounded Adonis."
    Cf. J. W. Lever, "Venus and the Second Chance", *Shakespeare Survey*, XV (1962), 81-88.

[42] See, for example, Michael Lloyd, "Cleopatra as Isis", *Shakespeare Survey*, XII (1959), 88-94.

[43] For a discussion of Cleopatra as both Dido and Hercules' Omphale, see Ernest Schanzer, *The Problem Plays of Shakespeare*: A Study of *"Julius Caesar"*, *"Measure for Measure"*, and *"Antony and Cleopatra"* (New York, Schocken Books, 1963), pp. 155 ff.

[44] Daniel Stempel, "The Transmigration of the Crocodile", *Shakespeare Quarterly*, VII (1956), 63-66 *passim*.

[45] See discussion, Chapter II.

sented more sympathetically than Octavius' merits has meaning in the drama. Never is an image examined within its context. Many of the images referring to Cleopatra's knowledge of poisons, for example, convey more of her knowledge of sexual "dying" than any pejorative connotations of witchcraft. The phallic qualities of serpents and worms are hardly esoteric. Although this kind of background study has given rise to the view that the play represents the struggle between Reason and Passion, *Antony and Cleopatra* has not received critical attention even in Lily B. Campbell's well-known *Shakespeare's Tragic Heroes: Slaves of Passion* [46] – perhaps because she felt that the play lacked the stature of the famous four, or that the Passion to which Antony and Cleopatra become slaves is not a decorous one.

The Elizabethan Attitude toward Cleopatra, or misogyny, or vation of women", an idea "familiar to all in Shakespeare's time" together with Dryden's comment that "the chief persons represented were famous patterns of unlawful love, and their end accordingly was unfortunate",[47] mirrors another commonplace of Elizabethan background studies of the play. Surely, speaking of The Elizabethan Attitude toward Cleopatra, or misogyny, or Passion is analogous to speaking of The Victorian Attitude or The High Renaissance Man. Characterizing The Elizabethan Attitude toward Jews, for example, is surely as difficult as characterizing The Twentieth-Century American's Attitude toward the Poles. Additional questions may provide answers to such an approach: Whose is The Elizabethan Mind? How typical an Elizabethan is Shakespeare? Is The View toward Women in the play necessarily Shakespeare's own? [48] Indeed we might suggest instead that a dramatic presentation of a number of sides of a philosophical

[46] Neither is the play considered in Hardin Craig, "Shakespeare's Depiction of Passions", *Philological Quarterly*, IV (October, 1925), 289-301.

[47] Dryden, Preface to *All for Love*, p. 229.

[48] Especially when we take into account the following contemporary ideas on the truth of poetry:

William Shakespeare, *As You Like It*: "the truest poetry is the most feigning" (III, iii, 19-20).

Cf. George Puttenham, *The Arte of English Poesie*, ed. Gladys Doidge Willcock and Alice Walker (London, Cambridge University Press, 1936), p. 40: "A fained matter or altogether fabulous, besides that it maketh

question is one of the characteristics of Shakespeare's method.[49]
Could not a single mind, moreover, if not that of an age, believe
simultaneously, for example, that the flesh was superficial and
ephemeral and yet a Platonic reflection of one's soul – especially
if that mind belonged to a poet and a dramatist?

Often the critic's love of *Antony and Cleopatra* is so removed
from the play that his unintentionally comic *dulce* completely
obscures any critical *utile*. The "Christian" critic, for example,
may reveal only his ideal of a "true Christian" (and how Shakespeare was just that), the staging critic may spend more time on
the monument (IV, xv) than in his study, and the textual critic,
we suspect, decries the lack of quartos. Everyone, whether atheist
or Catholic, would make Shakespeare his own. Yet surely even
Christians wince at criticism which claims that "Cleopatra's actions in the final act are in the main outlines comparable to those
of the penitent Christian",[50] or the rather un-christian view that
the "redemptions" of the play are "such as only a Christian poet
can understand".[51] Elizabeth Donno's reply to such criticism is
short and clear: "I submit that only by a wrenching of the poetic
and dramatic context can an explicit Christian scheme be imposed
upon *Antony and Cleopatra*. Of the Christian ethos of Shakespearian England, there is no question; one asks only that the
Shakespearian text be given its due." [52] Precisely for this reason,
I have endeavored to focus on Renaissance concepts of love,

---

more mirth than any other, works no lesse good conclusions then the most
true and veritable ...".

Sir Philip Sidney, "The Defense of Poesie", in *Literary Criticism* ...,
p. 424: "a feigned example hath as much force to teach as a true example ...".

Ben Jonson, "The Silent Woman", in *Works*, ed. C. H. Herford and
Percy Simpson (Oxford, Clarendon Press, 1925-52), prologue 2:

"... Poet neuer credit gained
By writing truths, but things (like truths) well fain'd".

[49] See discussion of "question structure", Chapter V.
[50] Cunningham, p. 14.
[51] J. A. Bryant, Jr., *Hippolyta's View. Some Christian Aspects of Shakespeare's Plays* (Lexington, University of Kentucky Press, 1961), p. 183.
[52] Elizabeth Story Donno, "Cleopatra Again", *Shakespeare Quarterly*, VI
(1955), p. 233.

sources, and parallels only when they are revealing of the text of
the play and the context of the scene.

The critics' love of *Antony and Cleopatra* has likewise been
dictated by the degree to which the views of love and life expressed in the play correspond to their own. Thus George Bernard
Shaw observes that "Shakespeare's *Antony and Cleopatra* must
needs be as intolerable to the true Puritan as it is vaguely dis-
tressing to the ordinary healthy citizen." "Besides", he adds, "I
have a technical objection to making sexual infatuation a tragic
theme. Experience proves that it is only effective in the comic
spirit." [53] Austin Wright arrives at a totally different view
through similar logical processes: "I consider the experience of
producing or viewing *Antony and Cleopatra* a salutary one for
young people of college age, who are all too prone to assume
that in the years of man as in a thermometer, 32 is the freezing
point." [54]

Equally personal are those critics whose passion for the play
depends on their love for Cleopatra as a woman outside the context of the play.[55] Even the women critics have become involved
in this manner, so that Rosa Grindon in "A Woman's Study of
Antony and Cleopatra" says that "the men critics [56] in their sym-

---

[53] Shaw, p. xxviii.

[54] Austin Wright, *"Antony and Cleopatra"* in *Shakespeare: Lectures on
Five Plays* by Members of the Department of English, Carnegie Institute
of Technology (Pittsburgh, Pennsylvania, Carnegie Press, 1958), p. 68.

[55] So many attacks upon Cleopatra's character have been made that a
few examples will suffice. Perhaps the most famous is the label of "courtesan of genius" given by Bernhard Ten Brink, *Five Lectures on Shakespeare*, trans. Julia Franklin (New York, Henry Holt and Co., 1895), p. 90.
The attacks, however, began long before Ten Brink and continued long
after him. Levin L. Schücking, for example, in *Character Problems in
Shakespeare's Plays* (New York, Henry Holt and Co., 1922), pictures her
as "a great courtesan" (p. 121). G. B. Harrison in his "Introduction to
Antony and Cleopatra" in his edition of *Shakespeare's Complete Works*
(New York, Harcourt, Brace and World, Inc., 1952) styles her "a magnifi-
cent courtesan" (p. 224). So numerous have been the attacks that Ralph
Behrens felt it necessary to write the very courtly "Cleopatra Exonerated!"
in *The Shakespeare Newsletter*, IX (November, 1959), 37.

[56] Mrs. Rosa Leo Grindon, "A Woman's Study of *Antony and Cleopatra*"
(Manchester, Sherratt and Hughes, 1909). Mrs. Grindon later calls these
"men critics" "obtuse as Enobarbus" (p. 68).

pathy for Antony, have treated Cleopatra just as Antony's men friends did, and for the same cause." [57] Mrs. Inchbald's rhapsodic explication of "Stands he, or sits he?" (I, v, 19) reduces to absurdity what so much of the criticism of the play has done with subtle sophistication: "Silly sentences to all who never were in love, but sensible, and most intelligent, to all who ever were." [58] Thus, if *Antony and Cleopatra* is, as some critics maintain, a rather shallow, though brilliant, explication of Reason and Passion, the critics have proven as frail as Antony in the battle with Reason. Perhaps it is this lack of reasonable explication of the text that accounts for *Antony and Cleopatra*'s being considered a "problem play." [59] Studies of the play have repeatedly provided more love than criticism.

---

[57] *Ibid.*, p. 9.
[58] Mrs. Inchbald, "Remarks" in *Antony and Cleopatra* (London, Longman, Hurst, Rees, and Orme, 1808), p. 4.
[59] Schanzer, see footnote 43, p. 18 above.

II

THE DANCER AND THE DANCE: A STUDY OF CHARACTERIZATION IN THE PLAY

Attention to Antony and Cleopatra as characters has usually passed for attention to *Antony and Cleopatra* as play. Whether or not the two have been considered gypsy and doting general, Venus and Mars, or Passion and Man, they have been viewed as if somehow the essence of their characters contained the essence of the play. Shakespeare's understanding of human nature has often been lauded,[1] but the resulting view of the tragedies as character studies of great men has seldom been challenged.

The chief objection to such a view of the plays is that it separates the character from the play of which he is but a part. Thus, in addition to such irrelevancies as "what confidence Shakespeare must have had in the boy actor for whom he wrote so subtle and rich a role"[2] as Cleopatra's, we have those studies which link Cleopatra with Shakespeare's alleged personal fascination for the dark-lady-Cleopatra before whom "every man is an Antony,

---

[1] See, for example, Schücking, *Character Problems in Shakespeare's Plays* and A. C. Bradley, *Shakespearean Tragedy* and *Oxford Lectures* above. Also see Leo Kirschbaum, *Character and Characterization in Shakespeare* (Detroit, Michigan, Wayne State University Press, 1962), and Frank Harris, *The Women of Shakespeare* (London, Methuen and Co., 1911).

[2] Theodore Spencer, "Preface" in William Shakespeare, *Antony and Cleopatra* (New York, Appleton-Century-Crofts, 1948), p. vii.

Cf. Harley Granville-Barker, *Prefaces to Shakespeare*, p. 125: Shakespeare "carefully ... avoids writing any scene in which a boy could not act without unpleasantness or in fear of ridicule".

Louis B. Wright and Virginia A. LaMar, "Egyptian Enchantress" in William Shakespeare, *Antony and Cleopatra* (New York, Washington Square Press, 1961), p. xiii: "Metaphor and suggestion take the place of visual love-making which would have been distasteful."

Shakespeare no less than another".[3] One critic flatly admits, "I definitely violate one of the standards of dramatic criticism in which I believe; I separate a character from the play in which this character is but one segment of the plot." [4] One example of this kind of separation, so characteristic of studies of the play, will suffice:

> If we now regard the Cleopatra of Shakespeare's drama we are astonished to find how inferior she is to the original. It is true that Plutarch gives us no clearly outlined picture of her character, but she certainly is not the great courtesan whom Shakespeare shows us in the first acts of his play. We are told nothing about her ability to negotiate with foreign peoples in their own language. As a matter of fact, we never see her acting as queen at all. Nobody would suspect that this woman, as Plutarch informs us, has, for years, quite unaided, ruled a great kingdom. She never gives audience, never exercises the function of her great office. Love seems to be her only aim in life.[5]

If Shakespeare's Cleopatra is inferior to Plutarch's as a person, she is surely not so as an artistic creation. Plutarch's creation is admittedly an indistinct "picture of her character". Indeed, by the same criterion, we might observe that Falstaff is inferior to

[3] Arthur Symons, *Studies in the Elizabethan Drama* (New York, E. P. Dutton and Company, 1919), p. 1.

Cf. Austin Wright, p. 45: "But Shakespeare feels Cleopatra's fascination, and one guesses that he was drawn to her against his will just as Antony was – and just as the poet had been to the heartless heroine of the sonnets."

Ivor Brown, *Shakespeare* (Garden City, New York, Doubleday and Company, 1949), p. 185: "The Dark Lady may or may not have been dead. But something snapped. The ecstasy and the agony were over."

Georg Brandes, *William Shakespeare. A Critical Study*, trans. William Archer and Mary Morison (New York, The Macmillan Company, 1899), p. 462: "Who knows! If he himself, William Shakespeare had met her, who knows if he would have escaped with his life?"

Neilson and Hill, p. 1245: "It could hardly have been insight alone . . . . If the richer music of *Antony and Cleopatra* does not invite recollection of the Sonnets, the amorous theme does, and it is conceivable that through his enigmatic Dark Lady, Shakespeare was assisted in imagining what Antony's Cleopatra was like."

See also Frank Harris, pp. 196-216 in which the "original" of Cleopatra is seen as Mary Fitton!

[4] Kirschbaum, p. 99.
[5] Schücking, p. 121.

Oswald, or that Hamlet would make an unsuitable roommate. If
Shakespeare's Cleopatra, unlike Plutarch's, "never gives audience,
never exercises the function of her great office", but seems to
have love as "her only aim in life", we might well ask why.
Rather than the implied rewriting of Shakespeare's play, a more
reasonable response would include the observation that the play
is not concerned with Cleopatra as a political figure, but with her
love for Antony.[6] While Shakespeare's varying from his source
may provide us with clues as to the emphases of the play, we
should, nonetheless, keep in mind Furness' admonition that it is
"necessary that we should accept Cleopatra, at SHAKESPEARE's
hands, with minds unbiased by history. We should know no more
of her than what we hear on stage. Of her past, of her salad days,
we should know nothing but what we are told." [7] The Dark Lady,
Plutarch's Queen, and Dante's damned "*Cleopatras lussuriosa*," [8]
are as irrelevant to Shakespeare's Cleopatra as Plutarch's or
Julius Caesar's Antony are to the Antony who loves Cleopatra.

Few even of the more recent studies of Shakespearean drama
have been exempt from separating character from play. Hamlet is
still equated with *Hamlet*. Despite his title of *Form and Meaning
in Drama*, H. D. F. Kitto emphasizes characterization in Elizabethan Drama, chiefly, however, to distinguish it from Greek
Tragedy (if indeed anything so broad as Elizabethan or Shakespearean Drama can be distinct). He carefully adds, "Not of
course that the Greek was philosophical with no interest in individuals, and the Elizabethan interested only in individuals with
no philosophical foundations: the difference lies in the balance
which each strikes between the two." [9] He draws the contrast yet
more strikingly, if less truly, later in his discussion: "More important, from our present point of view, is the fact that the minor

---

[6] See discussion, Chapter IV.
[7] H. H. Furness, "Preface" to William Shakespeare, *The Tragedy of
Anthonie, and Cleopatra* (Variorum Edition) (Philadelphia, Pennsylvania,
J. B. Lippincott, 1907), p. xi.
[8] Dante Alighieri, *Inferno*, V, 63 (Temple Classics Bilingual Edition)
(London, J. M. Dent and Sons, 1962).
[9] H. D. F. Kitto, *Form and Meaning in Drama: A Study of Six Greek
Plays and of "Hamlet"* (New York, Barnes and Noble, 1960), p. 209.

characters and subordinate incidents in the Elizabethan drama
have their independent reality. Launcelot Gobbo is not as important in the play as are Antonio and Shylock, but he is just as
'real'; we appreciate him for his own sake." [10] A negative approach
here yields a more precise insight into the characterizations in
the play. Launcelot Gobbo is no more real than Antonio,[11] whose
role in the play is more important than his, or Old Gobbo, whose
role is considerably less important (but none the less vital to the
artistic whole). He is obviously more caricature than characterization. Nor is Launcelot's lack of psychological reality intended
as a pejorative comment, for "the truest poetry is the most
feigning".[12] We do not look to comedies, even problem comedies,
for deep character studies. That we "appreciate him for his own
sake", we can partially agree; but that "the minor characters and
subordinate incidents in the Elizabethan drama have their independent reality", we cannot. Independent reality implies a
separation from the rest of the unified work of art. In II, ii, for
example, Launcelot is clearly not introduced "for his own sake".
During the course of his first speech alone he mentions the word
"conscience" ten times. The significance of the contrast between
Shylock's servant's conscience and Shylock's own is no less subtle
than effective. The dramatic sympathy that is directed away from
Shylock as his servant leaves him has more relevance in the play
than the credibility of a common servant using the word "conscience" ten times in a single speech. As a clown, his words and
actions are willingly believed within the context of the scene.
Although both he and the scene are comic in themselves, they

---

[10]   *Ibid.*, p. 223.
[11]   That Antonio is not a "psychologically real" character is clear from
the first lines of the play, in which he obviously speaks "out of character":

> In sooth, I know not why I am so sad:
> It wearies me; you say it wearies you;
> But how I caught it, found it, or came by it,
> What stuff 'tis made of, whereof it is born,
> I am to learn:
> And such a want-wit sadness makes of me,
> That I have much ado to know myself.
>   (*Merchant of Venice*, I, i, 1-7)

[12]   See discussion, Chapter I, footnote 48, p. 19 above.

have no "separate identity". Their only existence is that created by the artist within the artistic whole.

This lack of psychological probing, moreover, extends beyond the stock characters of comedy to the tragedies as well. While we can hardly question the sympathetic treatment of Ophelia and Cordelia, neither can we point to them as examples of full characterization. They are not called for in the emphases of the play. Whether or not Gertrude is guilty of the murder of Old Hamlet (or, if so, what her motives are) is a question which scholarly clubwomen have long debated, but with which *Hamlet* is relatively unconcerned. The repeated overemphasis of characterization in studies of tragedy leads us to ask whether the convention of shortening *The Tragedy of King Lear* to *King Lear* might not have more pejorative ramifications than its convenience warrants.

The "separate identity" of minor scenes and characters that Kitto speaks of has been applied to *Antony and Cleopatra*, perhaps most often in Cleopatra's messenger scenes (II, v; III, iii). The actions and reactions of the messenger, like those of Launcelot Gobbo, Charmian, Banquo, and Oswald exist as comparisons and contrasts to the actions and reactions of the protagonists. The interactions of these comparisons and contrasts compose the dramatic import of the play. To take these minor characters or scenes out of the context of the unified play distorts this meaning. By considering the separate identity of the messenger scenes, for example, some critics have been led to speak of Cleopatra's cruelty.[13] But the so-called cruelty all but vanishes within the context of the unified play. The effect of the scenes upon the spectator is one of Cleopatra's complete concern with Antony. Like Beatrice in *Much Ado* (I, i, 30-31; II, i, 7-10; cf. Benedick, I, i, 192 ff.; II, i, 209-210), she mentions her love at

---

[13] See, for example, John Holloway, *The Story of the Night: Studies in Shakespeare's Major Tragedies* (Lincoln, Nebraska, University Press, 1961), pp. 113-114: "Antony confirms his status as a gigantic outlaw among mankind by his treatment of Thyreus [or Thidias]. The ill-treatment of a messenger is as much a conventionalized act of decisive self-condemnation as Lear's division of the kingdom.... Cleopatra's ill-treatment of the messenger bringing news of Antony's marriage is plainly part of the same carefully-pointed sequence of events."

the least suggestion – even when it is a *non sequitur*. She begins her first scene with the messenger (II, v) by indirectly contrasting Antony's company with that of another woman or a eunuch. Fishing reminds her of catching Antonies. Charmian is reminded of a particular time that Antony and Cleopatra fished. Then Cleopatra remembers the many "times" (l. 18) she and Antony have had.

As if Shakespeare had not made the point of Cleopatra's love for Antony clear enough in the scene, Joseph Stull feels it necessary to read literal "Jewelry" into Cleopatra's figurative "merchandise" (l. 104), emphasizing her "magnanimity",[14] rather than her concern for the news that her love has remarried. But Cleopatra's first thoughts when the Messenger enters (like her first thoughts in the scene itself) are those of Antony:

> O, from Italy!
>
> *Enter a Messenger.*
>
> Ram thou thy fruitful tidings in mine ears,
> That long time have been barren.
>
> (ll. 23-25)

The forcefulness of her concern is underlined by the physical urgency of her word choices. The Messenger attempts to begin, but is interrupted by the anxious Queen:

> Antonius dead! – If thou say so, villain,
> Thou kill'st thy mistress: but well and free,
> If thou so yield him, there is gold, and here
> My bluest veins to kiss; a hand that kings
> Have lipp'd, and trembled kissing.
>
> (ll. 26-31)

Her impatience again dramatizes her love for Antony. The tone of her plea, moreover, recalls Rosalind's when Celia refuses to answer concerning Orlando (*As You Like It*, III, ii, 189 ff.), or Juliet's when the Nurse refuses news of her love (II, v).

Neither are Cleopatra's threats that she will "melt and pour"

---

[14] See Joseph Stull, "Cleopatra's Magnanimity: the Dismissal of the Messenger", *Shakespeare Quarterly*, VII (Winter, 1956), 73-78.

gold "down thy ill-uttering throat" (ll. 34-35) evidence of her cruelty. They demonstrate instead the intensity of her fear that Antony is dead. She does, after all, offer the Messenger "more gold" (l. 31) once he has told her Antony is well. She has already told us that her whole well-being depends upon Antony: "I am quickly ill, and well,/ So Antony loves" (I, iii, 72-73).

Cleopatra's cruelty within context, then, is as illusionary as that which Holloway sees when she exclaims that Antony "shall have every day a several greeting,/ Or I'll unpeople Egypt" (I, v, 77-78).[15] The speech emphatically dramatizes not her cruelty, but the firmness of her resolution, a firmness, moreover, which reflects the intensity of the love that motivates it. We need not follow Johnson's suggestion that Cleopatra means to unpeople Egypt "By sending out messengers"[16] in order to disprove Holloway's reading of cruelty. Neither need we accept Traversi's suggestion: "To 'unpeople Egypt,' should this be needed if she is to send daily messengers to Antony, is clearly as impossible as it would be irresponsible . . . ."[17] Nor need we point to other Shakespearean lovers sending daily greetings (in Sonnet 117 or "The Rape of Lucrece", l. 1289). The best commentary on the conscious exaggeration of her "I'll unpeople Egypt" is made clear by Cleopatra herself in III, xiii, when Cleopatra responds to Antony's question:

Ant. Cold-hearted toward me?
Cleo.   Ah, dear, if I be so,
From my cold heart leave heaven engender hail,
And poison it in the source, and the first stone
Drop in my neck: as it determines, so
Dissolve my life; the next Caesarion [18] smite
Till by degrees the memory of my womb,
Together with my brave Egyptians all,
By the discandying of this pelleted storm,

[15] Holloway, p. 113.
[16] Dr. Johnson, cited in the note to this line in The Variorium Edition of the play.
[17] D. A. Traversi, *Shakespeare: Tho Roman Plays* (London, Hollis and Carter, 1963), p. 106.
[18] See discussion, Chapter V.

> Lie graveless, till the flies and gnats of Nile
> Have buried them for prey!
>
> (ll. 158-167)

The coupling of "the memory of my womb" with both the maternally possessive "my" and the admiring "brave" illuminate the point in I, v, as well: not that she cruelly wishes to kill either her subjects or her children,[19] but that she loves them as much as she loves herself ("my neck") – indeed almost as much as she loves Antony.

The constant concern for Antony in II, v, moreover, is foreshadowed in I, v, when Alexas enters with a message and is greeted by

> How much unlike art thou Mark Antony!
> Yet coming from him, that great medicine hath
> With his tinct gilded thee.
>
> (I, v, 35-37)

Not only are eunuchs and women unlike Antony (II, v, 4 ff.), so are all other men. She bluntly informs the Messenger that "Hadst thou Narcissus in thy face, to me/ Thou wouldst appear most ugly" (II, v, 96-97), for he brings her news of Antony's marriage to Octavia. When he tells her of Octavia's faults (III, iii), however, she agrees with Charmian that he is "a proper man" (ll. 37-38). Again, all Cleopatra's actions and reactions are motivated by her thoughts of Antony.

While the obvious mirth that results when Cleopatra ("No more but e'en a woman", IV, xv, 73) "hales him up and down" (SD ff. II, v, 64) also lessens her supposed cruelty, it hardly lessens the intensity of her loving concern for Antony. Cleopatra herself, in a more reasonable moment, realizes that "These hands do lack nobility, that they strike/ A meaner than myself" (II, v, 82-83). The explanation for her actions is, of course, the *donnée* of drama, if not life, that "reason and love keep little company" (*A Midsummer-Night's Dream*, III, i, 147).[20] This same emphasis may be seen in Antony's whipping of Thidias, the "most kind

---

[19] G. B. Harrison, for example, in *Shakespeare's Tragedies* speaks of Cleopatra's supposedly "weak maternal feelings" (p. 224).
[20] See discussion of excess of reason below.

messenger" (III, xiii, 73) who kisses Cleopatra's hand, for here too the lover's jealous rage and the motivation for that rage overshadow the cruelty of the whipping. Although the whipping here is not applied by a woman, it is administered off-stage: "Take hence this Jack, and whip him" (III, xiii, 93). Cleopatra's gold (III, iii, 33), moreover, must mollify both messenger and spectator, by serving "to cure that blow of thine" (Cf. *Richard III,* IV, iv, 516). Antony's scene with Thidias hardly exists as "a separate incident", but derives and conveys part of its meaning from comparisons and contrasts with those of Cleopatra and her messengers. The chief similarity is the jealous and total love they feel for one another.[21] A contrast is further seen between Antony's insistence upon truth (I, ii, 95; I, ii, 102 ff.) and Cleopatra's attempts to create her own truth by prodding the Messenger to tell her only what pleases her.[22]

Thidias himself has no more separate identity than Charmian, Octavia, Caesar, or the very scene in which he appears. Surely Charmian, Mardian, Alexas, and Iras are more comic types than believable people, and both Octavia and Octavius are as wooden in characterization as in character. Their roles in the artistic whole supersede any attempt at characterization. Although they have not been often noted, the most obvious and recurring contrasts are those made between Charmian and Cleopatra. Just as the coarse bawdry of the servants in *Romeo and Juliet* contrasts with both the sophisticated sexual wit of Mercutio and the intense, naive passion of the lovers,[23] so do deliberate contrasts interact in *Antony and Cleopatra.* The urbane and bawdy wit of Enobarbus, the coarse and hilarious bawdry of Charmian and Iras, the sensual intensity of Antony and Cleopatra, and even the lack of all these in Octavia and Octavius comment dramatically upon one another. Charmian's own "worky-day fortune"

---

[21] See discussion of love and jealousy, Chapter IV.
[22] See Bryant for a discussion of the truth of nature *versus* the Truth of art as a theme in the play.
[23] See, for example, Mercutio's wit in I, iv, and II, iv. Contrast this physical stress with the idealized and religious language of the young lovers (e.g., I, v) and the coarseness of the language of the servants in I, i, and that of Peter and the Nurse in II, iv.

(I, ii, 52), like that she asks for Iras (l. 51), parallels the "dull world" (IV, xv, 61) which Cleopatra abhors. The proximity of the parallel argues for artistry over accident. Charmian, like Caesar, would be Fortune's knave (V, ii, 2-3), while Cleopatra desires

> To do that thing that ends all other deeds,
> Which shackles accidents, and bolts up change;
> Which sleeps, and never palates more the dung,
> The beggar's nurse, and Caesar's.
>
> (V, ii, 5-8)

The "worky-day fortune" of Charmian and Iras reminds us also of the one Cleopatra later envisions in Rome, once Antony is dead, "And there is nothing left remarkable/ Beneath the visiting moon" (IV, xv, 67-68), and in which

> ... mechanic slaves
> With greasy aprons, rules, and hammers shall
> Uplift us to the view. In their thick breaths,
> Rank of gross diet, shall we be enclouded,
> And forc'd to drink their vapour.
>
> (V, ii, 208-212)

Charmian's asking to "be married to three kings in a forenoon, and widow them all" (I, ii, 25-27), along with her specific request "to marry me with Octavius Caesar" (ll. 28-29) sharply contrasts the coarseness of both her prose and wishes with the poetry and actions of her mistress. Her exclaiming, "I love long life better than figs" (l. 32), moreover, differs from Cleopatra's wishes and actions concerning "long life" as well as "figs".[24] Yet another contrast is dramatized between Charmian, who "shall be more beloving than belov'd" (l. 22) and the beloved Cleopatra.

Another important contrast offers itself when Charmian's feelings for Julius Caesar conflict with those of her Queen. When Cleopatra asks, "Did I, Charmian,/ Ever love Caesar so?" she receives a rhapsodic "O that brave Caesar" and later "the valiant

---

[24] See "fig" in Eric Partridge, *Shakespeare's Bawdy: A Literary and Psychological Essay and A Comprehensive Glossary* (New York, E. P. Dutton and Co., 1960), p. 112. Even Partridge's "comprehensive glossary", however, fails to include the example here or in the basket in which Cleopatra finds her asps.

Caesar". Charmian persists, even after threats of receiving
"bloody teeth" for daring to compare Caesar with her mistress's
"man of men". It is Cleopatra, not Charmian, who speaks of her
love for Caesar as a result of the "green" judgment and "cold"
blood of her "salad days" (I, v. 66 ff.). Cleopatra, moreover, has
already admonished Charmian by declaring it "treason" to say
that she thinks of Antony "too much" (ll. 6-7). The contrast between Charmian and Cleopatra here strongly resembles that between Juliet and the Nurse concerning Romeo and Paris:

Nurse.   Faith, here it is.
    Romeo is banish'd; and all the world to nothing
    That he dares ne'er come back to challenge you;
    Or, if he do, it needs must be by stealth.
    Then, since the case so stands as now it doth,
    I think it best you married with the County.
    O, he's a lovely gentleman!
    Romeo's a dishclout to him. An eagle, madam,
    Hath not so green, so quick, so fair an eye
    As Paris hath. Beshrew my very heart,
    I think you are happy in this second match,
    For it excels your first; or if it did not
    Your first is dead; or 'twere as good he were
    As living here and you no use of him.
                    (III, v, 214-227)

Juliet cannot believe the all-too-reasonable "comfort" and
"counsel" and asks, "Speak'st thou from thy heart?" Once the
Nurse replies, "And from my soul too; else beshrew them both",
Juliet's "Well, thou hast comforted me marvellous much", assumes a meaning for the audience unlike that understood by the
Nurse. The Nurse is no more heroic than Charmian (although
no less reasonable than Octavius), and tragedies are not made of
their stuff. But they do serve to direct the course of the audience's
sympathy toward Juliet and Cleopatra. This surely is the kind of
parallel that Coleridge had in mind when he proposed that *Antony
and Cleopatra* "should be perused in mental contrast with *Romeo
and Juliet*",[25] with which it composed "Shakespeare's double portrait of Love".[26]

[25] Coleridge, I, 86.
[26] *Ibid.*, II, 319.

Charmian's very first giddy words with Alexas, moreover, immediately following the first scene with Antony and Cleopatra, distinctly differ from Cleopatra's toward Antony: "Lord Alexas, sweet Alexas, most any thing Alexas, almost most absolute Alexas" (I, ii, 1-2). Neither does Alexas' own comment that "if it lay in their hands to make me a cuckold, they would make themselves whores" (ll. 73-74) provide mere filler for the scene. Again a contrast is asked for between Cleopatra and her servants. The Queen, once choosing Antony as her spiritual "Husband" (V, ii, 286), never considers cuckolding her dead husband by submitting to another man. Iras' choice of her "inch of fortune" somewhere other than her husband's nose (ll. 55 ff.) lacks the poetry of Cleopatra's response to Antony:

> I would I had thy inches, thou shouldst know
> There were a heart in Egypt.
>
> (I, iii, 40-41)

The very tone of the verse glimpsed in the decorous "thou" and majestic "Egypt" stands in direct opposition to the coarse comedy of Iras. Cleopatra's reply, with the suggestiveness of poetic art, provokes at least several readings: "I would I were a man, for in a man's role, I could tell you of my love"; "I wish that I had thy inches in height, then I should be both taller and in command"; and "I desire thy inches in an erotic sense, for at that moment you'd know that the Queen of Egypt is a passionate woman who loves you."

But if the actions and reactions of the minor characters comment upon those of the protagonists, this does not suggest that Antony and Cleopatra have any more "separate identities" than their servants. Shakespeare's Antony and Cleopatra have life only within the confines of the play itself (if so "spacious" a play may be termed "confined"). Whether or not they are either worthwhile or psychologically believable people outside the play is irrelevant. Indeed, even within the play itself we are asked to consider a number of views of the lovers.[27]

---

[27]　Cf. William Rosen, *Shakespeare and the Craft of Tragedy* (Cambridge, Massachusetts, Harvard University Press, 1960), p. 105: "The most im-

In addition to studies of Antony and Cleopatra as people, there are those in which the main characters are viewed as they adhere to Aristotelian concepts of "hero." That Renaissance commentaries on and translations of Aristotle abound is common knowledge to Renaissance scholars.[28] That Shakespeare's protagonists are not bound by Aristotle's descriptive criticism of Greek Tragedy seems less well-known. Perhaps because "tragic heroes" are easier to discuss — Aristotle supplies us with such useful classroom-discussion words as *anagnorisis, hamartia,* and *peripeteia* — most approaches to *The Tragedy of Antony and Cleopatra* have been through its protagonists. Most of these pseudo-Aristotelian studies, however, assume that the play is "the story of Antony".[29] Indeed, one critic suggests that "the play would have been better entitled *The Decline and Fall of Antony*".[30] Although such a limited view of the play reveals little awareness of either theme or tone, let us not concern ourselves with titles, for they are, especially in Shakespearean drama, outside of the artistic whole.

As if to answer the male critic above, Lucie Simpson states that "the play, in fact, might have been called *Cleopatra* as ap-

---

portant reason why *Antony and Cleopatra* has been interpreted in so many ways is that we, as audience, are constantly forced to change our point of view."

See discussion "question structure", Chapter V.

[28] See Bernard Weinberg, *A History of Literary Criticism in the Italian Renaissance* (Chicago, University Press, 1961). 2 Volumes. Four chapters (IX-XII) are devoted to the influence of Aristotle's *Poetics* alone.

[29] Hardin Craig, *An Interpretation of Shakespeare,* p. 268.

Cf. Willard Farnham, *Shakespeare's Tragic Frontier. The World of his Final Tragedies* (Berkeley, University of California Press, 1950), p. 175: "Shakespeare does not organize his tragedy as a drama of the love of Antony and Cleopatra, but as a drama of the rise and fall of Antony in the struggle for world rulership that takes place after he has met Cleopatra."

John F. Danby, *Poets on Fortune's Hill. Studies in Sidney, Shakespeare, Beaumont and Fletcher* (London, Faber and Faber, 1952), p. 146: "For the tragedy of *Antony and Cleopatra* is, above all, the tragedy of Antony."

See discussion of Structure, Chapter V.

[30] Lord David Cecil, p. 21.

propriately as Hamlet is called *Hamlet* or Othello *Othello*".[31] But *Antony and Cleopatra,* of course, is no more about Cleopatra than *Hamlet* is merely about Hamlet. While we are prone to deride earlier notions of the tragedies as character studies, we still hear *Hamlet* spoken of most often as the story of a man who procrastinates and *Richard II* as the story of a poet who could not be King. We still approach the plays in the classroom through such Aristotelian terms as *hamartia*. We know not what else to do with them.

Undoubtedly the strongest argument against such an emphasis on characterization, however, derives from Aristotle himself. While Aristotle does mention character as one of the six parts which compose every tragedy, he lists it second in importance. The parts he mentions, of course, are "plot, character, diction, thought, spectacle, and music".[32] That character is not the exclusive concern of Tragedy, Aristotle makes clear:

The most important of these is the putting together of the separate actions, for tragedy is an imitation not of men but of actions and life. And happiness and unhappiness reside in action, and the end is some sort of action, not a quality, for according to their characters men are what they are, but according to their actions they are happy or the reverse. They do not, then, act in order to represent character, but in the course of their actions they show what their characters are; so in the actions and the plot is found the end of tragedy, and the end is more important than anything else. Besides, without action there can be no tragedy, but without characters there can be one. The tragedies of most recent writers are deficient in character, and in general the same thing is true of many poets.[33]

He quickly defines character as "that which reveals an agent's moral habit, showing of what sort it is",[34] before proceeding to his discussion of "the arrangement of incidents", which, he reiterates, is "the first and most important matter in tragedy".[35]

---

[31] Lucie Simpson, "Shakespeare's 'Cleopatra' ", *Fortnightly Review*, CXXIX (March, 1928), 332.
[32] Aristotle, *Poetics*, trans. Allan H. Gilbert in *Literary Criticism*, p. 77.
[33] *Ibid.*
[34] *Ibid.*, p. 79.
[35] Sir Philip Sidney, "The Defense of Poesie", in *Literary Criticism*, p. 427.

This same emphasis on plot underlies Sidney's description of the poet, "with a tale forsooth he cometh unto you",[36] and the ballad-making minstrel immediately comes to mind as predecessor and comrade of the poet. Indeed, the tale seems often to be the structural *dulce* by which the dramatist captures the spectator in order to show him the *utile*.

Unfortunately, however, Aristotle's descriptive comments on the nature of Greek tragic heroes have become more widely known than his comments on the relative importance of character:

With respect to the characters there are four things it is necessary to aim at. The first is that they be good. There will be character, as has been said, if speech or act clearly shows a moral choice indicating what sort of person an agent is; his character will be good if his choice is good. There is goodness in every type of person, for a woman is good and so is a slave, though one of these is perhaps inferior, the other paltry. The second necessity is that character be appropriate, for there is a manly character, but it is not fitting for a woman to have a masculine character or to be powerful.[37] The third necessity is that character have resemblance.[38] For this is something else than to make characters good and appropriate, as has been said above. The fourth necessity is that character be consistent. For if a character is not consistent because the man who is imitated was such a character, nevertheless it is necessary that he be consistently inconsistent.[39]

Even in introductory courses in Shakespeare, then, we are likely to hear such questions as: "Does Macbeth become so immersed in evil that he can no longer be a tragic hero?" "Does Othello satisfy Aristotle's demands for tragic stature?" "Does Hamlet achieve *anagnorisis* or does he remain an ignorant instrument of Providence?" "If he does not achieve this tragic recognition, is the tragedy deficient?" The questions are viewed as central to the

[36] See discussion of Cleopatra's "masculinity" and Antony's supposed "effeminacy", Chapter IV.
[37] *Ibid.*, p. 78.
[38] Resemblance to what, Aristotle does not explain. Gilbert in his note to the line suggests "mythic prototypes" as one possibility. Indeed, the reading is lent authority by what Aristotle says later in the *Poetics* of metaphor: "this alone cannot be learned from others and its use is a sign of genius, for to use metaphors well is to see resemblance" (p. 103).
[39] Aristotle, pp. 89-90.

play's meaning, and Aristotle's descriptions are seen as demands.

Aristotle himself would surely be aghast at the application of his criticism to Shakespeare's black-sheep tragedy, *Antony and Cleopatra*. It is almost as if Shakespeare were maliciously attempting to foil those who would approach his play from a strictly Aristotelian point of view. The play is nominally and integrally about two people instead of one – and one of these is a woman. The two, moreover, indulge in what some Elizabethans and some twentieth-century scholars consider deadly sin, although "of the deadly seven it is the least" (*Measure for Measure*, III, i, 111). Perhaps because he was less aware of Medieval and Elizabethan background than some recent scholars, Shakespeare – or rather *Antony and Cleopatra* – does not categorically place his lovers (like Francesca and Paolo [40]) in the *Inferno*. The question of love's sinfulness is one of the questions of the play.[41]

While the Aristotelians have catalogued such references as "Egypt", "Venus", "Mars", and "Demi-Atlas of the world", too often to warrant another such list, we must not be led to believe that the play utilizes the terms only to demonstrate the tragic stature of its protagonists. The comparisons with Venus and Mars, for example, connote more about love than about "men of high reputation and good fortune, such as Oedipus and Thyestes and famous men of similar families".[42] This is not to suggest that Antony and Cleopatra are common folk, but that their tragic stature depends less on earthly rank than on their symbolic [43] implications. In Cleopatra's name as well as Antony's "lay/ A moiety of the world" (V, i, 18-19). The utilization of Aristotle's definition of hero to judge all Shakespearean protagonists, moreover, not only ignores the domestic dramatic tradition, Shake-

---

[40]   Dante, *Inferno*, V, 73 ff.
[41]   See Brents Stirling, *Unity in Shakespearian Tragedy. The Interplay of Theme and Character* (New York, Columbia University Press, 1956), p. 159: "It is interesting that Shakespeare seems to have anticipated the problem of sexual infatuation as a tragic theme by actually posing the question as a theme in the play."
   Cf. discussion of "question structure", Chapter V.
[42]   Aristotle, p. 86.
[43]   See discussion below.

speare's uniqueness as artist, and that of the play itself, but also mistakes descriptive criticism for prescriptive and goes on to place it above creative art.

One of the problems created by imposing Aristotelian criteria upon the play is the view that in spite of their earthly and meta-phorical stature, Antony and Cleopatra are "conceived in essen-tially non-heroic terms", and "encased in a heroism of words which do not integrate with the action itself".[44] This same critic even suggests that we inquire "whether the cosmic images in *Antony and Cleopatra* do not appear, at least to a certain extent, forced and imposed upon rather than integrated with the central theme".[45] The critics who note the "inadequacy" of Antony and Cleopatra as Aristotelian tragic heroes also view them as having little rapport with the audience [46] – even that they are laughable.[47] The problems are those of the critics, however. The audience is unaware of them. We have to remember only Macbeth, if not Antony and Cleopatra themselves, to realize that dramatic sym-pathy is something quite apart from life. Surely they, more than Macbeth, occupy "the mean between saintliness and depravity".[48] In both *Macbeth* and *Antony and Cleopatra,* one point becomes clear: that with Shakespeare,[49] as with Aristotle, plot came before character.

In *Antony and Cleopatra* this sympathy becomes not only more relevant than such concepts as tragic stature and *hamartia,* but more revealing. Whether the decisions of Antony and Cleo-patra are complete "errors" is a question raised, but not decided, in the play. We as audience would hardly have them do otherwise.

---

[44] Nicoll, p. 152.

[45] Rosen, p. 133: "A. C. Bradley and Arthur Sewell are dissatisfied with him [Antony] because little rapport exists between protagonist and au-dience."

[46] Maynard Mack's preface to his edition of *Antony and Cleopatra* (Bal-timore, Maryland, Penguin Books, 1960), p. 15.

[47] *Ibid.*

[48] Aristotle, p. 86. See also p. 86n.

[49] Cf. E. E. Stoll, "Cleopatra", *Modern Language Review*, XXIII (1928), 151: "Plot came first with the poet [Shakespeare], not, as the critics often say and continually imply, the central character. The action gave birth to the character, not the character to the action."

Indeed, the soothsayer (so consistently important in Elizabethan and Greek Tragedy) advises Antony to leave Octavius' side:

> Therefore, O Antony, stay not by his side:
> Thy demon, that thy spirit which keeps thee, is
> Noble, courageous, high, unmatchable,
> Where Caesar's is not. But near him, thy angel
> Becomes afeard; as being o'erpower'd, therefore
> Make space enough between you.
>
> (II, iii, 17-22)

Almost without exception the play directs our sympathy toward Antony and Cleopatra and away from Octavius and his sister. Octavius himself, in a speech praising Antony after his death, is as aware as the Soothsayer and the audience that "we could not stall together,/ In the whole world" (V, i, 39-40).

Easily the most obvious way in which Shakespeare directs our sympathy in favor of the judgments of the lovers is through a dramatic [50] contrast with Octavius Caesar. Caesar's judgments, nonetheless, are those some critics would have Antony and Cleopatra make in order to qualify them as suitable Aristotelian heroes. They are not those that we as audience and participants in the drama would have them make. If, for example, Octavius is unlike Antony in being immune to the charms of Cleopatra, so is Mardian (I, v, 9-12). And Mardian is a quite unheroic eunuch. Indeed, even in her carefully prepared scene with Seleucus, Cleopatra feels it necessary to suggest that her Treasurer is less than a man not to have remained adoringly loyal to her. "Wert thou a man", she chides him, "Thou wouldst have mercy on me" (V, ii, 173-174). When Caesar asks, "Which is the Queen of Egypt?" (V, ii, 111) we hardly think of his question as heroic. We must consider him either stupid and unfeeling not to recognize so rare a creature, or an insolent boy to be rude to Cleopatra so soon after Antony's death. When Cleopatra calls him "Sole sir o' the world" (l. 119), we can only chuckle at her conscious irony, for she has just told us she considers it "paltry to be Caesar" (l. 2). The contrast asked for in the text between this boyish "Sole sir"

---

[50] The word "dramatic" as used in this study means that which we see and hear on the stage as it interacts with the rest of the play.

and her literally unique "Arabian bird" (III, ii, 12) needs no
Richard Burbage [51] to capture the sympathy of the audience. The
contrast, moreover, becomes yet more ludicrous when we measure
"the young Roman boy" (IV, xii, 48) with the dream proportions
the Emperor Antony has now attained by which his legs bestride
the ocean and his face is as the heavens (V, ii, 76-100).

Indeed, we sympathize more with the drunken Lepidus (II,
vii, 4; II, vii, 90 ff.) than we do with the abstemious Caesar.
Lepidus' condition, by its extremity as it mirrors Antony's own,
also serves to prevent our bringing "Antony ... drunken forth"
(V, ii, 217-218) with any humorously degrading connotations.[52]
Neither is Caesar's lack of participation in the festivities left to
the staging. The text itself affirms it in Caesar's own words:

> What would you more? Pompey, good-night. Good brother
> Let me request you off: our graver business
> Frowns on this levity. Gentle lords, let's part,
> You see we have burnt our cheeks. Strong Enobarb
> Is weaker than the wine, and mine own tongue
> Splits what it speaks: the wild disguise hath almost
> Antick'd us all. What needs more words?
>   (II, vii, 118-124)

In fact the wild disguise of wine has "antick'd" all but Caesar,
and Antony, if foolish, is also sympathetically human. Caesar's
refusal to continue drinking with the others demonstrates not the
isolation of the tragic hero who needs must act his dismal scene
alone (Cf. *Romeo and Juliet*, IV, iii, 19), but the unsympathetic
non-participant who thinks that because he is "virtuous, there
shall be no cakes and ale". Drink, moreover, like lechery, is a

---

[51] Although there is no actor list or direct knowledge of the first performances recorded in any contemporary diary, it is more than probable
that Richard Burbage played the role of Antony. The DNB gives Burbage's
dates as 1567?-1619 so that he would have been alive and about the right
age for the part. It is well-known that he "had all the best parts" (as the
DNB states). Burbage is also assigned the role in Thomas Whitfield Baldwin, *The Organization and Personnel of the Shakespearean Company*
(Princeton, University Press, 1927).

[52] Lepidus, then, absorbs by his extremities the pejorative aspects of
Antony's condition, much as Edgar's assumed and fantastical madness ac-
complishes the same dramatic purpose in Lear's mad scenes.

universally manly, social sin. Like love, it belongs to the particular realm of the soldier.[53] Indeed, they are surely heroic sins,
when compared to gluttony and sloth, for example. While Falstaff's lack of honor and love of anarchy, gluttony, and sloth
may argue against him, the social nature of his drinking demands
the sympathy of the audience. It is a tradition of both life and
literature (which too seldom agree) that we sympathize not only
with lovers,[54] but also with "one that loves a cup of hot wine with
not a drop of allaying Tiber in't" (*Coriolanus*, II, i, 52-53).

The contrast between the manner in which Antony and Caesar
behave toward Lepidus also directs our sympathy toward Antony
and away from Caesar. Because Antony

> frets
> That Lepidus of the triumvirate
> Should be depos'd, and being, that we detain
> All his revenue,
>
> (III, vi, 27-30)

he is dramatically contrasted not only with Caesar, who speaks
these lines unapproving of his behavior, but also with his own
actions after Enobarbus deserts him (IV, v). When Caesar invites
only Antony "to my sister's view" (II, ii, 167), Antony generously
remembers the third pillar of the world (weak though it be) and
thoughtfully adds, "Let us, Lepidus,/ Not lack your company"
(II, ii, 168-169). The effect of this generosity upon the audience
is voiced by Lepidus himself, who replies to the "Noble Antony"
(II, ii, 169). The deliberateness of the contrast is underscored by
Antony's criticism of Lepidus in *Julius Caesar*:

---

[53] Robert Burton, *The Anatomy of Melancholy*, ed. Rev. A. R. Shilleto
(London, G. Bell and Sons Ltd., 1903-1916), III, 40. While Burton in his
anatomy of the lover's melancholy mentions the soldierly virtue of love,
the association of the soldier with "love" is still a common one.
[54] Francis Bacon, "Of Love" in *Works*, ed. James Spedding *et al.* (London, Longmans and Co., 1870-72), VI, 397, observes that "the stage is
more beholding to Love, than the life of man". Plato in *The Symposium*,
trans. B. Jowett (Boston, International Pocket Library, [n.d.]), however,
mentions the "encouragement which all the world give to the lover" (p. 41).
He even speaks of "the entire liberty which gods and men allow the
lover ..." (p. 42).

This is a slight unmeritable man,
Meet to be sent on errands; is it fit,
The threefold world divided, he should stand
One of the three to share it?

                    (IV, i, 12-15)

But these are the words of a young Antony – another play, "another Antony" (V, ii, 350).

At two specific points in the play, when we know for certain that what Caesar says is not true, our sympathy is directed toward Antony when it might well be elsewhere. Caesar says, for example,

Why have you stol'n upon us thus? You come not
Like Caesar's sister: the wife of Antony
Should have an army for an usher, and
The neighs of horse to tell of her approach,
Long ere she did appear. The trees by the way
Should have borne men, and expectation fainted,
Longing for what it had not. Nay, the dust
Should have ascended to the roof of heaven,
Rais'd by our populous troops: but you are come
A market-maid to Rome, and have prevented
The ostentation of our love; which, left unshown,
Is often left unlov'd: we should have met you
By sea, and land, supplying every stage
With an augmented greeting.

                    (III, vi, 42-55)

Here we might easily sympathize with him in feeling that his sister is a "cast-away" (l. 40). But, we, like Octavia herself, know that he has no cause (l. 41) to do so. When she replies, "To come thus was I not constrain'd, but did it/ On my free will" (ll. 56-57), our remembrance of Antony's parting words verifies her claim:

                              Provide your going,
Choose your own company, and command what cost
Your heart has mind to.

                    (III, iv, 36-38)

In addition to the contrast between Octavia's entrance and the Cleopatra-like one that Caesar dreams for his sister (in which

expectation should have fainted "longing for what it had not"),
the lengthy speech deliberately undercuts any wrong we might
feel concerning Antony's unseen flight to Cleopatra. Another
contrast between Octavia and Cleopatra presents itself in Octavia's arrival as a "market-maid to Rome," and Cleopatra's dying
to avoid such an arrival there. The connotations of "market-maid"
here are clearly pejorative, for Octavia lacks the self-awareness
that accompanies Cleopatra's description of herself as

> No more but e'en a woman, and commanded
> By such poor passion as the maid that milks,
> And does the meanest chares.
>
> (IV, xv, 73-75)

We are also aware of the lack of truth in Caesar's statement to
Lepidus:

> You are too indulgent. Let's grant it is not
> Amiss to tumble on the bed of Ptolemy,
> To give a kingdom for a mirth, to sit
> And keep the turn of tippling with a slave,
> To reel the streets at noon, and stand the buffet
> With knaves that smell of sweat: say this becomes him, –
> Whom these things cannot blemish . . . .
>
> (I, iv, 16-23)

Although Caesar disbelieves it, we are to learn that Antony is
"rare indeed". We note it in Agrippa's statement that "A rarer
spirit never/ Did steer humanity" (V, i, 31-32). He is truly an
"Arabian bird" (III, ii, 12). The audience, moreover, might easily
respond, as Lepidus does that Antony's faults do indeed "become" more than they "blemish" him:

> I must not think there are
> Evils enow to darken all his goodness:
> His faults, in him, seem as the spots of heaven,
> More fiery by night's blackness.
>
> (I, iv, 10-13)

More important, we realize that Caesar is wrong again. It is not
in the sweaty streets at noon that Antony reels, but at night and
alone with his love. There is no tippling slave. We have already
heard Antony specifically say to Cleopatra, "And all alone/ To-

night we'll wander through the streets, and note/ The qualities of people" (I, i, 52-54). The differences noted here are hardly trivial. Antony speaks of wandering Arabian-night-fashion in the evening more like "A little touch of Harry in the night" (*Henry V*, prologue, IV, 47) than the indecorous mixing with Bardolph or a tippling slave. It is no accident that the *persona* in Vaughan's famous poem saw Eternity "the other night",[55] rather than in the realistic, sweaty day. Night is the time for lovers as well as mystics. The fact that he and Cleopatra are going to "note/ The qualities of people" surely excludes any mingling with slaves. It is in North's Plutarch, not in Shakespeare's play, that Antony wanders "disguised like a slave" (accompanied by Cleopatra "in a chambermaid's array") peering into poor men's windows.[56] Shakespeare's Cleopatra, moreover, far more than Caesar, makes clear her disgust with both sweat and slaves, when she says,

> Mechanic slaves
> With greasy aprons, rules, and hammers shall
> Uplift us to the view. In their thick breaths,
> Rank of gross diet, shall we be enclouded,
> And forc'd to drink their vapour.
>
> (V, ii, 208-212)

Both Antony and Cleopatra are also compared and contrasted with the eunuch Mardian. With Antony and Cleopatra as well as with Mardian, these dramatic comparisons supersede any deep, psychological probing – indeed, they form the very characterizations in question.[57] So exclusively concerned is the play with Mardian's lack of sex that at one point he is called "Photinus, an eunuch" (III, vii, 14).[58] His role's the thing. The contrast of

[55] Henry Vaughan, "The World" in *Works*, ed. L. C. Martin (Oxford, Clarendon Press, 1914), l. 1. Cf. *Romeo and Juliet* in which Juliet is both a "bright angel" (II, ii, 26) and "the sun" (II, ii, 4). But love is its own light and abhors the day (III, v, 1-41).

[56] Plutarch, "The Life of Marcus Antonius", trans. Sir Thomas North from Amyot's French and ed. by C. F. Tucker Brooke in *Shakespeare's Plutarch* (New York, Duffield and Company, 1909), II, 44.

[57] Cf. Aristotle, p. 77: "They do not, then, act in order to represent character, but in the course of their actions they show what their characters are ...".

[58] See also III, vii, 14n. Note in addition that Shakespeare often designates profession or role (e.g., clown, constable, mother), rather than name.

Antony (and indirectly of Cleopatra) with Mardian begins before their very first entrance on stage. The contrast is dramatic, as we hear Philo say that "Antony is become the bellows and the fan/ To cool a gypsy's lust" (I, i, 9-10), and then see what follows in the original stage direction that continues the scene:

Flourish. Enter ANTONY, CLEOPATRA, *her Ladies, the Train, With Eunuchs fanning her.*

Surely with so conscious a craftsman as Shakespeare, the textual and palpable fan offers no accidental comparison. While it may at first seem strange to compare the virile Antony with a eunuch, it is a paradox of life and literature that that which most easily proves a man "masculine" may most easily subdue and unsex him. It is a paradox that the play dramatically presents more than once in the play.[59] More often, however, Mardian the eunuch (and the word is repeatedly used in the play, even as an epithet, e.g., I, v, 7) by contrast directs our attention to the physical attractiveness of Antony (I, v, 7-18; II, v, 3-9).

Enobarbus, as reasonable as Mardian and Caesar, but wittier and more feeling, also directs dramatic sympathy toward Antony. Although he has choric functions, Enobarbus is also a character. This is one of the differences in "balance" that Kitto speaks of between Elizabethan drama and Greek Tragedy. Aristotle himself advises the combination: "The chorus should be treated as one of the actors, should be an integral part of the whole, and should participate in the action . . . ."[60] What Enobarbus says and when he says it are more dramatically significant than whether or not his speeches are either consistent or psychologically believable. He speaks almost omnisciently when he tells us that "men's judgements are/ A parcel of their fortunes" (III, xiii, 31-32). Neither is he "in character" in his ironic condemnation of his later actions when he describes his present ones:

> He that can endure
> To follow with allegiance a fall'n lord,

[59] See for example, Antony's "She has robb'd me of my sword" (IV, xv, 23) immediately after Mardian enters.
[60] Aristotle, p. 97.

Does conquer him that did his master conquer,
And earns a place i' the story.
(III, xiii, 43-46)

Yet he is also a character to be himself judged by the audience (with the assistance of his own choric tongue) as "alone the villain of the earth,/ And feel I am so most" (IV, vi, 30-31). That Enobarbus here serves as a contrast to direct the audience's sympathy toward Antony is made clear by his following line:

O Antony,
Thou mine of bounty, how wouldst thou have paid
My better service, when my turpitude
Thou dost so crown with gold?
(IV, vi, 31-34)

Enobarbus as character remains completely unaware, when he says, "No, I will go seek/ Some ditch wherein to die: the foul'st best fits/ My latter part of life" (IV, vi, 37-39), that he provides a dramatic contrast in this ditch with that which Cleopatra will later propose:

Shall they hoist me up,
And show me to the shouting varletry
Of censuring Rome? Rather a ditch in Egypt
Ben gentle grave unto me, rather on Nilus' mud
Lay me stark-nak'd, and let the water-flies
Blow me into abhorring; rather make
My country's high pyramides my gibbet,
And hang me up in chains.
(V, ii, 55-62)

Cleopatra's choice is a ditch to an ignoble life, while Enobarbus' ditch is a punishment for an ignoble choice. This ignominy, then, contrasts with the nobility (V, ii, 284) and majesty (V, ii, 279) of Cleopatra's death, and the contrast dramatically and deliberately comments on the play's themes.

While Enobarbus' reasonable nature may at times cause him to be as sympathetic as Horatio, there are more things in heaven and earth than are dreamt of in their philosophies. *Antony and Cleopatra* dramatizes some of these "things". It is this very lack of the foolhardy and foolish in both Enobarbus and Horatio that

prevents them from attaining the stature of a Hamlet, a Prometheus, an Antony, or a Cleopatra. While the reasonable man becomes Fortune's knave (V, ii, 3), Prometheus steals from the very
gods, and Antony and Cleopatra "do that thing that ends all
other deeds,/ Which shackles accidents and bolts up change . . ."
(V, ii, 5-6). Whether or not the tragic hero succeeds in defying
order, or the gods, or Fortune, matters little. Perhaps it is "impossible". But tragic heroes are those who make the attempt,
regardless. The reasonableness of the cynical Enobarbus, who
must be reprimanded for his "light answers" (I, ii, 174), becomes
relevant in the evaluation of his comments. It is his reason and
cynicism that heightens the attraction of Cleopatra, for despite
his joking of Cleopatra's "business" (I, ii, 171) and bawdy punning
on women's dying, he delivers both the famous barge speech (II,
ii, 191 ff.) and the equally famous one that soon follows:

> Age cannot wither her, nor custom stale
> Her infinite variety: other women cloy
> The appetites they feed, but she makes hungry,
> Where most she satisfies. For vilest things
> Become themselves in her, that the holy priests
> Bless her, when she is riggish.
>
> (II, ii, 235-240)

Shakespeare, not Plutarch, assigns the speeches to Enobarbus.
Neither would Enobarbus wish that Antony "had never seen her"
(I, ii, 150), for he "had then left unseen a wonderful piece of
work, which not to have been blest withal, would have discredited
[his] travel" (I, ii, 151-153). That Enobarbus here speaks in prose
hardly undercuts the poetic force of the feeling with which the
values of the play ultimately agree. The audience would no more
have Antony banish this "wonderful piece" [61] than it would have
Hal "banish plump Jack, and banish all the world" (*I Henry IV*,
II, iv, 526-527). Falstaff and what he represents are as important
for Hal to experience in his growth to Henry V as Cleopatra and
what she represents are to Antony's growth to dream proportions
(V, ii, 74 ff.). Cleopatra, moreover, unlike Falstaff, who is neces-

---

[61] See "piece" in Partridge's glossary. The word could mean more than
simply "masterpiece". Cf., for example, *Titus Andronicus*, I, iii, 309.

sarily discarded, herself grows to dream proportions (V, ii, 288-289; V, ii, 344-346).

That even this utterly reasonable man feels Cleopatra's attractions not only emphasizes her fascination, but also serves to underscore the unsympathetic, almost unnatural restraint of Mardian and Octavius. They alone are immune to her. The point is not that Octavius is a eunuch, but that in terms of the values of the play he is unsympathetically, excessively reasonable. Thus while Lily B. Campbell's famous study admirably sets forth the thesis that Shakespeare's tragic heroes are slaves of passion,[62] no study of either the comedies or the tragedies has delved deeply into the problem of excess of reason. Yet the excess of reason pervades both. We may note it, for example, in Lear's diabolical daughters, whom he must admonish to "reason not the need" (II, iv, 267), but rather to respond to natural, human feelings. Perhaps the most fully developed example of extreme reason without feeling is the unnatural Angelo, who, the Duke tells us, "scarce confesses/ That his blood flows, or that his appetite/ Is more to bread than stone . . ." (Measure for Measure, I, iii, 51-53). So unnatural is the extremity of his reason that Lucio even suggests "this Angelo was not made by man and woman after this downright way of creation (III, ii, 111-112), but "was begot between two stock-fishes" (III, ii, 116). So inhuman is he that he is spoken of as "a man who blood/ Is very snow-broth" (I, iv, 57-58) and one, who "when he makes water his urine is congealed ice" (III, ii, 117-118). Extreme reasonableness in a lover, of course, belongs only to the comedies – and even there only to the rejected one.[63] Shakespeare's satire of those who recognize only man's angelic reason without acknowledging his animal appetites is also seen in such characters as Malvolio and Jacques. The attitude of the audience toward the unsociable pair is well reflected in their

---

[62] See Lily B. Campbell, *Shakespeare's Tragic Heroes: Slaves of Passion* (New York, Barnes and Noble, 1960).
[63] See, for example, "I am glad this parcel of wooers are so reasonable, for there is not one among them but that I dote on his very absence, and I pray God grant them a fair departure" (Portia in *Merchant of Venice*, I, ii, 118-121).

devastatingly comic names.[64] If Jacques is last seen going to the "abandon'd cave" (*As You Like It*, V, iv, 202) and Malvolio is "notoriously abused (*Twelfth Night*, V, i, 388) and promising revenge (V, i, 386), Angelo joins the final festivities of the comedy only because of Marianna's feelings for him, not because of his own reason. Only "by her election may be truly read/ What kind of man he is". While the line is from *Cymbeline*, the idea that "all he needs is a nice girl" is one central to the comic view. It is equally true in literary and theatrical tradition that sympathy resides with lovers [65] (whether or not Cleopatra is a "nice girl" matters not). While physical love may be less reasonable than angelic reason, it is an heroic fault, and if the "gods will give us/ Some faults to make us men" (*Antony and Cleopatra*, V, i, 32-33), what more heroic and universally sympathetic fault could they select?

Indeed, we might argue that sympathy is least with Antony when his reason proves him unfeeling toward Cleopatra. We hardly sympathize with his speaking of his hours with her as "poisoned" (II, ii, 90) or of the Queen herself as "a boggler ever" (III, xiii, 110), a "foul Egyptian" (IV, xii, 10), or a "Triple-turned whore" (IV, xii, 13). Regardless of our willingly suspended personal judgments concerning Cleopatra, Antony's words here, like Cleopatra's actions earlier, "lack nobility" (II, v, 82). We surely admire the pair most when they are suffering at the bottom of Fortune's wheel. We are well aware that Jupiter's statement; "Whom best I love I cross" (*Cymbeline*, V, iv, 101), is as relevant to Antony and Cleopatra as it is to Prometheus and Oedipus. It is a concept central to Tragedy that "Nothing almost sees miracles/ But misery" (*King Lear*, II, iii, 172-173).

If Enobarbus, Mardian, and Caesar direct sympathy chiefly toward Antony, Octavia directs our sympathy chiefly toward Cleopatra. If Octavia is wronged, and surely she is, that is only half the story. That she is "of a holy, cold, and still conversation"

---

[64] The many Elizabethan puns on "jakes" even in the heroic "Ajax" are common and are still, of course, made on the modern equivalent of "a john". See "jakes" in Partridge.

[65] See discussion above.

(II, vi, 119-120), we have Enobarbus' word. The play makes clear from the beginning of her forced marriage that it is no love match; Antony married "but his occasion here" (II, vi, 128-129). While Cleopatra's "something it is I would" (I, iii, 89) implies the intensity of her emotion, Octavia sounds somewhat silly in her analogous inability to communicate:

Oct. Sir, look well to my husband's house; and —
Caes.   What,
      Octavia?
Oct.   I'll tell you in your ear.
Ant. Her tongue will not obey her heart, nor can
      Her heart inform her tongue — the swan's down feather,
      That stands upon the swell at the full of tide,
      And neither way inclines.
                          (III, ii, 45-50)

By inclining neither way, like one of Dante's trimmers,[66] this "swan's down feather" surrenders the dramatic sympathy that a Desdemona, for example, gains by replying to her father that while she recognizes "a divided duty" (*Othello*, I, iii, 180), yet

            here's my husband;
  And so much duty as my mother show'd
  To you, preferring you before her father,
  So much I challenge that I may profess
  Due to the Moor, my lord.
                    (ll. 185-189)

Even the comic Hermia defies the command of both her father and Theseus in order to wed Demetrius (*A Midsummer-Night's Dream*, I, i). She gives her father the same forceful reason in the precedent set by her mother and wins the approval of the audience. Ultimately, the play shows her choice to be "the right one" (Elizabethan attitudes toward arranged marriages notwithstanding).

We should, nonetheless, agree with John Holloway's assertion that

A marriage to cement an alliance need have nothing cynical, shameful, or dishonourable about it;[67] and the play gives no reason what-

---

[66] Dante, *Inferno*, III.
[67] Holloway here is "answering" Traversi, *An Approach to Shakespeare*, pp. 244-245.

ever to suppose that the "helpless sister Octavia" either was helpless in respect of her devoted brother (Shakespeare seems to follow Plutarch here), or would have wished to help herself in any way other than by furthering his wishes. Attitudes like this may have become obsolete, but they are neither incomprehensible nor unattractive.[68]

Later, however, when speaking of Plutarch's account of Octavia as "the most fortunate woman on earth . . . wife and sister of the two great commanders", Holloway adds, "These attitudes are nearer to Shakespeare's by far than those of today." [69] This is the danger of background studies. Shakespeare's personal attitude is both unknown and irrelevant. Regardless of The Elizabethan Attitude toward arranged marriages, we have already noted the sympathetic treatment of Hermia's and Desdemona's refusal to adhere to them. The audience's sympathy is as clearly with Cleopatra as it is with Juliet. Octavia and Paris have little of this sympathy. We rarely even see Octavia and she has no spokesman, as Cordelia does, in Kent or the Fool. When we do see Octavia, we hear little that proves any profound love for Antony (see, for example, II, iii, 1-9). In Dryden's play, she meets Cleopatra. In Shakespeare's she is not even comparable. When Cleopatra's messenger leads her to believe what she wants to believe of Octavia (that she is "dull of tongue, and dwarfish", III, iii, 16), we laugh with Cleopatra and at Octavia. When Cleopatra in the final scene of the play speaks of "dull Octavia", we must agree with her. In spite of her infrequent presence on stage, Octavia is surely one of those women who "cloy/ The appetites they feed . . ." (II, ii, 236-237). And a lack of sympathy for her causes us to muse that despite the brevity of her role in the play, "None ever wished it longer than it is." [70]

Cleopatra's ability to "make hungry,/ Where most she feeds" (II, iii, 237-238), on the other hand, represents the audience's attitude as well as Antony's. This is still true at the play's end. Even on Antony's deathbed, she pleases both him and the audi-

[68] Holloway, pp. 110-111.
[69] *Ibid.*, p. 111.
[70] Cf. Samuel Johnson on *Paradise Lost* in "Life of Milton" in *Lives of the English Poets*, ed. George Birkbeck Hill (Oxford, Clarendon Press, 1905), pp. 183-184.

ence by her playfulness. Some seem to prefer the whining of an Octavia, and complain of Cleopatra's selfish cruelty [71] when she asks,

> Noblest of men, woo't die?
> Hast thou no care of me, shall I abide
> In this dull world, which in thy absence is
> No better than a sty?
>
> (IV, xv, 59-62)

Yet within the context of the scene, her speech is as playful as that in which she says, "Here's sport indeed! How heavy weighs my lord!" (IV, xv, 32). The loving (rather than cruel) nature of her playfulness becomes apparent when we note that her purpose is to save Antony his breath (ll. 42-43), and when we contrast it with the intense sorrow with which she breaks forth once he is dead (ll. 64 ff.). We care not for the "dull Octavia", who is undoubtedly a part of the "dull world" of which Cleopatra speaks. The playfulness adds pathos rather than cruelty to the scene, just as the punning of Mercutio (III, i, 100-102) and Gaunt (*Richard II*, II, i, 82) increases the pathos of their death scenes. Would we instead, with the cruelty of Richard II, ask, "Can sick men play so nicely with their names?" (II, i, 84).

Cleopatra, moreover, pictures Antony as the "noblest" of men, just as she does in her discussion of Julius Caesar with Charmian (I, v, 66 ff.). Octavia, on the other hand, divides her love between Antony and Octavius:

> A more unhappy lady,
> If this division chance, ne'er stood between,
> Praying for both parts:
> The good gods will mock me presently,
> When I shall pray, "O, bless my lord, and husband!"
> Undo that prayer, by crying out as loud,
> "O, bless my brother!" Husband win, win brother,
> Prays, and destroys the prayer, no midway
> 'Twixt these extremes at all.
>
> (III, iv, 12-20)

To be certain that this "love is not love/ Which alters when it

[71] See discussion of Cleopatra's "cruelty" above.

alteration finds" (Sonnet 116), we have only to remember Juliet's contrasting words after Romeo has killed Tybalt (III, ii). Juliet can divide her love no more than Cleopatra. While, out of the context of the play, one could easily argue for the selfish and cruel Cleopatra as opposed to the loyal Octavia of the golden mean, the tone and context argue otherwise. The extent of the deliberate direction of our sympathy toward Cleopatra is reflected not only by such omissions as Octavia's pregnancy in Plutarch,[72] but also such additions as Cleopatra's erroneous forecast that in Fulvia's death she sees how hers will be received (I, iii, 65-65). When Antony hears Mardian report Cleopatra's death, he does indeed echo the very words he speaks when he hears of Fulvia's death (Cf. I, ii, 154-157 and IV, xiv, 34).[73] But the words and actions that follow Antony's speech contrast his deeper love for Cleopatra with that he feels for either Octavia or Fulvia. We are shown little, if any, of these "loves".

In Shakespeare's play this dramatic sympathy and tone are of more relevance than character-probing or *hamartia*. Indeed, the comic tone created by the foolishness of the protagonists, by which some would deny them tragic stature,[74] strongly contributes to their heroism. In addition to directing our sympathy toward them by making them more human, their foolishness is often foolhardy and daring. Like Coriolanus' entering the city "alone/ To answer all the city" (I, iv, 51-52), Antony dares Caesar to single combat "sword against sword,/ Ourselves alone" (III, xiii, 27-28). Caesar prudently and unheroically refuses (IV, i, 4-6). Again when Antony and Cleopatra foolishly agree to fight by sea (III, vii, 27-28), when even a common soldier realizes the necessity to fight by land (III, vii, 60 ff.), we feel a sense of heroism in their foolish defiance. Even when Antony's daring extends to raging, "I would they'ld fight i' the fire, or i' the air,/ We'ld fight there too" (IV, x, 3-4), we feel we have witnessed the bravado of a Hotspur in his excess of passion. Neither raging madness, dotage, nor foolishness, moreover, can categorically deny Antony and Cleopatra

[72]   Plutarch, II, 54.
[73]   Cf. I, ii, 115 for the first time Fulvia's death is reported.
[74]   See discussion below.

their tragic stature. All three elements are present in another who is both a tragic hero and "every inch a king". Perhaps it is an awareness of this foolishness as an essential ingredient of tragic heroes from Prometheus to Antony that has led many to translate *hamartia* as "error in judgment" rather than "tragic flaw". Cleopatra foolishly jabbers with Mardian. She argues with Charmian. She talks of Antony and catching fish. She even beats a messenger. But her foolish lack of reason dramatizes her complete love of Antony, even after his death. Would we have her give way to Antony in all things, and reasonably cross him in nothing (I, iii, 9)? If so, she might well respond to us, as to her serving maid, "Thou teachest like a fool: the way to lose him" (l. 10). Charmian's advice is Octavia's way. Even on her own deathbed, Cleopatra foolishly becomes jealous that Antony will make demand of Charmian, "and spend that kiss/ Which is my heaven to have" (V, ii, 301-302). But her jealousy proves her love.[75] Cleopatra's supposed selfishness here, like Antony's clumsy death earlier, have been pointed to as undercutting their stature. But in the context of the play, their foolishness gains our sympathy and reflects their love. Their most flagrant foolishness, moreover, their defiance of Fortune, demonstrates that the foolishness itself heightens their stature.

Rather than studies of tragic stature or *hamartia* or psychological reality, then, studies of the characterizations of Antony and Cleopatra should include a summation of what we see and hear them do and say in the light of comparable and contrasting actions. This interaction forms their dramatic characterizations.[76] When Austin Wright, then, proposes that "the main theme" of *Antony and Cleopatra* is not probing into the character of either Antony or Cleopatra, but into "the clash between Antony and Octavius",[77] he does note at least one of the interactions of the play. When Lord David Cecil, however, adds that "the love story is seen always in its relation to the rivalry between Octavius and

---

[75] See discussion of love and jealousy, Chapter IV.
[76] See footnote 57, p. 45 above.
[77] Austin Wright, p. 39.

Antony",[78] we note (as in Wright's terming this relation "the main theme") that the emphasis of the play is shifted from the lovers to Antony and Octavius. No one in the audience ever shifts the focus of the play from Antony and Cleopatra. The shift comes only from "study". Both Octavius' and Octavia's love for Antony depend on Antony's love for Cleopatra. The very use of such love terms as Caesar's speaking of Antony as "my mate in empire" (V, i, 43), moreover, when multiplied in the play,[79] demonstrates that the emphasis is not on Antony and Octavius, indeed not on Antony and Cleopatra as people, but on love. The danger of the view that "the central theme of *The Tragedy of Antony and Cleopatra* is the relationship of Antony and Cleopatra" [80] is the extension that the focus of the play is on "the purely personal relations of the lovers" [81] and lacks "the public nature" of *Julius Caesar* or *Coriolanus*.[82] *Antony and Cleopatra*, like *The Winter's Tale, The Tempest*, and *Timon of Athens* (rather than the so-called Roman Plays with which it is consistently grouped), is more symbolic than either personal or public.

While Hazelton Spencer has argued that "Antony and Cleopatra are too well-known to be ideal tragic figures: they resist the symbolizing tendency of all serious and poetic drama",[83] other critics have equated Cleopatra, for example, with Isis,[84] Ceres,[85] Lilith,[86] "Eve and the serpent in one",[87] Omphale,[88] Venus,[89] "everlasting woman",[90] or Antony's "absolute", "his heart's desire

---

[78]   Lord David Cecil, p. 13.

[79]   See discussion of love and empire, Chapter IV.

[80]   L. C. Knights, "On the *Tragedy of Antony and Cleopatra*", *Scrutiny*, XVI (1949), 318.

[81]   M. W. MacCallum, *Shakespeare's Roman Plays and Their Background* (London, Macmillan and Co., 1910), p. 339.

[82]   Lord David Cecil, p. 14.

[83]   Hazelton Spencer, p. 341.

[84]   See Michael Lloyd, "Cleopatra as Isis".

[85]   *Ibid.*

[86]   Edward Dowden, *Shakspere. A Critical Study of His Mind and Art* (New York, Harper and Brothers, 1900), p. 313.

[87]   Brandes, p. 462.

[88]   Maizitis, pp. 142 ff.

[89]   *Ibid.*, pp. 144 ff.

[90]   Algernon Charles Swinburne, *A Study of Shakespeare* (New York, R. Worthington, 1880), p. 191.

made perfect".[91] The difficulty comes in the equation. Antony is no more Mars, Adam, or Hercules, than Cleopatra is Venus, Eve, or Omphale. But the comparisons are made in the play. We can speak more precisely of the "allegorical bent" [92] of *Antony and Cleopatra* than speak of it as an allegory.

The most common failing in the approach to the play, however, has not been the exclusion of the personal level of the lovers, but the exclusion of all else. Dr. Johnson, for example, viewing the play from the literal plot alone, objects to its lack of characterization:

Except the feminine arts, some of which are too low, which distinguish Cleopatra, no character is very strongly discriminated. Upton, who did not easily miss what he desired to find, has discovered that the language of Antony is, with great skill and learning, made pompous and superb, according to his real practice. But I think his diction not distinguishable from that of others: the most tumid speech of the play is that which Caesar makes to Octavia.[93]

Rather than a failing in characterization, the lack of distinguishable diction and any real soliloquies [94] demonstrates instead Shakespeare's symbolic method in the play. This it not to say that the servants and protagonists speak the same language, which Kitto points to as a characteristic of Greek Tragedy.[95] While we do not focus exclusively on the universal aspects of the characters of Antony, Cleopatra, or Antigone, for example, we do note a difference in the "balance" Kitto mentions. We are concerned as

[91] Bradley, *Oxford Lectures*, p. 297.

[92] Geoffrey Bush, *Shakespeare and the Natural Condition* (Cambridge, Massachusetts, Harvard University Press, 1956), p. 129.

[93] Johnson, X, 212-213.

Cf. Bethell, pp. 117-118: "The employment of such imagery is not limited to one or two personages in the play, but is characteristic of them all. There is, in fact, no attempt to differentiate character by the verse they speak, except to some extent with Octavius Caesar, whose verse is normally dull and flat and impersonal, or else staccato as he issues orders. But when he speaks of Antony, or Cleopatra, of the Empire, his verse too takes on the grandeur and dignity met with in the others. . . ."

[94] Enobarbus [pseudonym for Steele Commanger], "The Imagery of *Antony and Cleopatra*" (Harvard College, Winthrop Sargent Prize, 1954), p. 5.

[95] Kitto, p. 229.

reader or spectator with Antony and Cleopatra both as lovers and
as symbols. That Antony and Cleopatra are historical figures,
gives dramatic substance to the symbolic story presented. The
combination is significant:

It is not that the Greek tragic poets were too high-minded "corruptly
to gratify the people"; the satyric play did nothing else than to serve
this reprehensible purpose. But if we go back to the fundamental
difference between the Greek and the Elizabethan drama we find a
very natural explanation. We argued that a background of ordinary
life is an essential part of Elizabethan drama; that it is one of the
means by which the central action is given solidity and reality. . . .
Since introduction of the comic and the low – Eastcheap, gravediggers,
jesters – helps us to feel that the play is "true to life," for here is the
tragic action, surrounded by life.[96]

The individual natures of Antony and Cleopatra, then, participate
in and comment on the symbolic nature of the play of which they
are a part. But the characters themselves are both individual and
symbolic. The individuality is attested to by their historical basis
and their unique excellence: Cleopatra as "A lass unparallel'd"
(V, ii, 315) and Antony as the "Arabian bird" (III, ii, 12) or
phoenix. Neither does this individuality exclude their symbolic
or universal nature. Cleopatra is both that Queen of Egypt unlike
all other women who cloy the appetites they feed, and "No more
but e'en a woman, and commanded/ By such passion as the maid
that milks,/ And does the meanest chares" (IV, xv, 73-75).
Antony is both the greatest soldier in the world and "the abstract
of all faults/ That all men follow" (I, iv, 9-10). And they are
more. Only the play can contain their infinite variety. No study
should even presume to do so.

The most common fault of character studies of Antony and
Cleopatra, however, has not been to attempt too much, but to
exclude either their individual or symbolic nature. Those who
insist on interpreting all Shakespeare's tragic protagonists as
psychologically believable characters might well object to the in-
sincerity or hypocrisy of either Othello's oft-quoted blank verse
assertion that "Rude am I in my speech,/ And little bless'd with

[96]   *Ibid.*

the soft phrase of peace..." (I, iii, 81-82) or Henry V's felici-
tously phrased prose apologies to Katharine for being similarly
awkward (V, ii). The different dramatic effect of the speeches is
attested to by the tone of the passages and the reaction of the
audience. Few in the audience worry about either consistency or
consistent inconsistency. When an idea is to be introduced into
a play, one of the characters on stage does so. It may or may not
be "in character". Antony as character, for example, may have
no idea that "These strong Egyptian fetters I must break,/ Or
lose myself in dotage" (I, ii, 113-114), but we as audience must
be introduced to and prepared for this idea at this time. Antony,
likewise no more knows at the time that "though I make this
marriage for my peace,/ I' the east my pleasure lies" (II, iii, 38-
39) than Hal at another moment knows

> you all, and will a while uphold
> The unyok'd humour of your idleness.
> Yet herein will I imitate the sun,
> Who doth permit the base contagious clouds
> To smother up his beauty from the world,
> That when he please again to be himself
> Being wanted, he may be more wond'red at
> By breaking through the foul and ugly mists
> Of vapours that did seem to strangle him.
>   (I Henry IV, I, ii, 218-226)

Indeed, in character, Hal might well be charged with a prideful,
if not bombastic, self-comparison with the sun. While it is not
contradictory to believe Cleopatra as character is aware both that
she is "with Phoebus' amorous pinches black,/ And wrinkled
deep in time" (I, v, 28-29) and that the Messenger who has seen
her "hath seen some majesty" (III, iii, 41), it is more an awareness of the play than a self-awareness that she demonstrates when
she says

> Be it known, that we, the greatest, are misthought
> For things that others do; and when we fall,
> We answer others' merits in our name,
> And therefore to be pitied.
>   (V, ii, 175-178)

Antony's sudden reversals of love and hate of Cleopatra are no

more to be questioned as to consistency of character than Aufi-
dius' sudden "My rage is gone" (*Coriolanus*, V, vi, 148), which
follows his equally sudden aside against Corialanus (V, ii, 200-
202). We are not asked whether or not they are consistent: our
judgments are willingly suspended and we are shown.

Commenting on those who would view Cleopatra purely as a
believable character study, S. L. Bethell exclaims, "No wonder
Cleopatra's character worries the psychologist; it is not so much
a character as an extended metaphysical conceit." [97] He says that
for this reason in his "treatment of the 'character' of Cleopatra...
I tried to show that we were not so much concerned with psy-
chology, as with the concrete poetic description of a complex
interpretation of experience". But in his treatment, unfortunately,
Bethell seems to discard his "not so much" and the individuality
of the lovers to proclaim that "Octavius Caesar stands for the
Roman qualities as Cleopatra does for the Egyptian", and that
"Octavia is the translation of Rome into woman".[98] But Cleopatra also "stands for" the historical Queen of the Nile, just as
Octavia also "is" the second wife of Antony and the sister to
Octavius. Much like Isabella in *Measure for Measure*, they function as both character and symbol. An exclusion of either level
renders any study deficient. Isabella is surely "out of character"
when as a kind of allegorical mercy she can say (without fear of
egotism), "You do blaspheme the good in mocking me" (I, iv,
38). But she is hardly inconsistent when as character (and but a
human reflection of the qualities she symbolizes), she exclaims,
"O, I will to him and pluck out his eyes!" (IV, iii, 124) or un-
mercifully cries out for "justice, justice, justice, justice" (V, i,
25). In much the same way Falstaff is both "the reverend vice"
(*I Henry IV*, II, iv, 499) and Hal's companion, and the Fool in
Lear is both jester and "Lear's shadow" (I, iv, 251). So then
Antony is Phoenix, Adam, and Cleopatra's "man of men", just
as she is both the only woman who cloys not Antony and "no
more but e'en a woman". The two, then, function as both char-

[97]   Bethell, p. 132.
[98]   *Ibid.*

acter and symbol. Neither symbol nor character, however, exists except as a part of the unified play. The dancers are but a part of the dance.

III

WORLD IMAGERY, COMEDY, AND BAWDRY: THEIR FUNCTIONS IN THE LOVE THEME

Rhapsodic vagueness and separation from the artistic whole have dominated studies of the imagery as well as studies of the characters of *Antony and Cleopatra*. The separation is clear in the seminal work on Shakespeare's imagery by Caroline Surgeon. In *Shakespeare's Imagery and What It Tells Us*, Miss Spurgeon catalogues the images in an attempt to discover "the many ways" by which Shakespeare "so magically stirs our emotions and excites our imagination".[1] Although "sometimes", she tells us, her method of study "even throws light on the significance of the play concerned", what is "most important of all" is "the way Shakespeare himself saw [the imagery]".[2] With the biographical slant we dismissed as irrelevant to studies of characterization, she admittedly focuses on Shakespeare's life, or a single tone in a play, as the end to her cataloguing. Her approach, unfortunately, has proved more seminal than her industry. That tone may bear on a play's meaning or that a number of tones may simultaneously be present in a play has not been considered by many critics. The single tone that Miss Spurgeon sees as "dominating" the infinite variety of tones in *Antony and Cleopatra*, for example, is the spacious grandeur created by its "world" or "colossal" imagery:

The group of images in *Anthony and Cleopatra* which, on analysis, immediately attracts attention as peculiar to this play, consists of images of the world, the firmament, the ocean and vastness generally.

---

[1] Caroline Spurgeon, *Shakespeare's Imagery and What It Tells Us* (Boston, Massachusetts, Beacon Press, 1958), p. 355.
[2] *Ibid.*

That is the dominating note in the play, magnificence and grandeur, expressed in many ways. . . .[3]

Critical views of the dominating tone of the play, however, have varied from the sublimely holy to the ridiculously corrupt. Ironically, identical passages from the play have been offered as "evidence" for dominating tones that Traversi would term "mutually exclusive". Yet those who have viewed the play as colossally spiritual have been as extravagantly exclusive in their claims as those who would have the entire play characterized by corruption and decay. Miss Pogson at one extreme, for example, suggests that "the union of the peerless twain is a representation of Transcendental Love, of Divine Union, which was enacted in the outer world of history, and later on the European stage, as an ideal to which man might aspire".[4] Pointing to many of the same erotic passages as do those who view the play as corruptly bawdy, Miss Pogson explains that

the language of physical love has often been used in religious poetry to describe the joy of Divine Union. It is the language of the Song of Songs, of the Sufi poems, of the lyrics of the troubadours, and Shakespeare follows in the train of the Hebrew, Persian, and Provençal mystics, taking as his subject one of the most glorious histories of love that are recorded in order to illustrate a mystical experience.[5]

Using the imagery of the play as a footnote to support her preconceived conclusions, rather than analyzing it in context, Miss Pogson compares, for example, the silver, gold, and purple of Cleopatra's barge (II, ii, 191 ff.) with the same colors in Solomon's chariot, and its perfume (l. 193) with "the goodly fragrance of the sacred ointments".[6] Enobarbus' description of the barge in the play, however, offers no hint to the comparison.

Whether the critics have regarded the imagery as holy or decaying, they have usually agreed that the end of the imagery is "atmosphere". That Shakespeare's plays when staged by his con-

---

[3] *Ibid.*, p. 350.
[4] Beryl Pogson, *In the East My Pleasure Lies. An Esoteric Interpretation of Some Plays of Shakespeare* (London, Stuart and Richardson, 1950), p. 107.
[5] *Ibid.*, p. 108.
[6] *Ibid.*, pp. 108-109.

temporaries lacked elaborate scenery and relied on imagery is a critical commonplace. That Shakespeare's plays rely on imagery for ideas as well is not. Thus, just as the night images in *Macbeth* have been explained as necessary for an afternoon performance of a murder presented in the open, so have the world images of *Antony and Cleopatra*[7] been shown as necessary to create a spaciousness on the confined Elizabethan stage (in the manner of the *Henry V* prologues). Indeed, some would have the sensuous imagery of the play justified by the indecorous alternative of a sensuous boy actor.[8] Two of the better studies of the imagery of the play, those of Clemen and Charney, do at least go one step beyond atmosphere. "Thus Shakespeare's imagery", Clemen explains, "which at first glance seems only to create the atmosphere of the play, actually affects more than this. It is symbolically related to the characters, serves their self-interpretation and the expression of their feelings."[9] That Clemen approaches the play with Aristotelian criteria is glimpsed in his statement that "the main theme of the play, the fall of the great lovers, is metaphorically expressed".[10] Charney makes his critical agreement clear by emphasizing both "tragic stature" and the fall of Antony in the titles of his final sections on "the function of the imagery of the play": "The Heightening of Cleopatra", and "The Tragedy of Antony". Indeed, tragic stature has seemed the sole end of catalogues of the gods, demigods, and world images of the play.[11] Thematic possibilities have been ignored or discounted.

While Daiches in "Imagery and Meaning in *Antony and Cleopatra*" obviously considers the thematic implications of the play's images, he focuses solely on the individual's assumed roles in his

---

[7] See, for example, Spurgeon, pp. 350 ff.; Knight, pp. 206 ff.; and Maurice Charney, *Shakespeare's Roman Plays. The Function of Imagery in the Drama* (Cambridge, Massachusetts, Harvard University Press, 1961), pp. 79-93.

[8] See discussion, Chapter I.

[9] Wolfgang Clemen, *The Development of Shakespeare's Imagery* (New York, Hill and Wang, [n.d.]), p. 162.

[10] *Ibid.*

[11] See discussion, Chapter II.

search for identity.[12] By ignoring an exploration of this concept within the framework of the love theme, Daiches neglects, for example, the paradoxical search for individuality through union, which is also dramatized in the play.[12] Bryant also admirably attempts to analyze the world images thematically, but his emphasis on "unifying action", Christian implications, and the poetic dream of Hippolyta's view leads him as well to neglect the play's context of love. Despite Bryant's convincing assertion, for example, that Antony's dream proportions are poetic in nature and do indeed demonstrate Cleopatra's attempt "to catch an image of human dignity",[14] we must surely take issue with his emphasis on this as the unifying and central element of the play. When Cleopatra strives to "catch another Antony/ In her strong toil of grace" (V, ii, 345-346), she is surely more concerned with love than with human dignity. The image she creates of the Emperor Antony (V, ii) is not so much a product of "the poet", as Bryant suggests, but of "the lover" (A Midsummer-Night's Dream, V, i, 7), who is as integral a part of Hippolyta's view as the poet. It is not so much poetic art as "the art of love" that is responsible for Cleopatra's creation of the Emperor Antony. Because the love of the artist for the work he creates is emphasized in the vision of the play (cf. Homer's "children"), the emphasis of the play seems to be focused less on Nature versus Art, as Bryant would have it[15] than on Reason or "Reality" versus Love and Art. It is Shakespeare more as the Poet of Love, Ovid Metamorphosed,[16] than simply the Bard, who presents a new Antony created by Cleopatra's love to inhabit the "new heaven, new earth" (I, i, 17) of Love. The world images of the play, then, thematically dramatize the creative possibilities of the "lunacy" of love, a lunacy

---

[12] See David Daiches, "Imagery and Meaning in Antony and Cleopatra", English Studies, XLIII (1962), 343-358.
[13] See discussion below.
[14] Bryant, p. 174.
[15] Ibid., p. 176. Bryant emphasizes such lines as II, ii, 200-201; II, ii, 218; and V, ii, 96 ff. Cf. Knight, pp. 257 ff. Traversi, The Roman Plays, p. 115.
[16] Francis Meres, Palladis Tamia. Wits treasvry being the second part of Wits common wealth (London, P. Short for Cuthbert Burbie, 1598), p. 282: "the sweete wittie Soule of Ouid lives in mellifluous & hony-tongued Shakespeare ...".

which enables Antony and Cleopatra by the end of the play to "stand up peerless" (I, i, 40). Octavia and Caesar, like the Reasonable Theseus, are but a part of that "world to weet" (l. 39), and thus never attain any but the literal proportions Dolabella would grant Antony. Indeed, Dolabella is so reasonable that he understands Cleopatra's question (V, ii, 93-94) no more than Theseus understands Hippolyta's reply.

Some of the difficulty of the studies of world images arises from the very grouping of the images to illustrate any single effect. Thus in this same first scene when the question of the peerless nature of Antony and Cleopatra is raised, it would be a mistake to view Cleopatra's declaration, "I am Egypt's queen" (l. 29), merely as a footnote to her stature. As we have repeatedly seen in our discussion of characterization, context is all. Here, for example, Cleopatra continues and adds, "Thou blushest, Antony, and that blood of thine/ Is Caesar's homager" (ll. 30-31). Within the context of the scene, then, Cleopatra as Queen asserts an independence of Caesar and Fulvia that Antony cannot, an independence or sovereignty, moreover, that is to form a major motif in the play.[17] Antony and Cleopatra in the course of the play must defy not only Caesar, as the Soothsayer tells Antony (II, iii, 10 ff.), but even Fortune (V, ii, 2 ff.).[18] The context that is all, then, is not merely the context of the scene, but of the entire play. The world images, like the other images of the play, accrue meanings as they interact with those that precede and follow them in the play.[19] These interactions form an essential "drama" within the macrocosm of the play.

One of the interactions of the world imagery which Bryant's unifying action ignores is the gigantic proportions of Antony's past (as well as those of his potential greatness) [20] with the present

---

[17] See Daiches above, and discussion below.
[18] See discussion of love and Fortune, Chapter IV.
[19] Cf. Rosemund Tuve, *Elizabethan and Metaphysical Imagery. Renaissance Poetic and Twentieth-Century Critics* (Chicago, University Press, 1961), p. v: "All comments on images taken in isolation seem to me invalid."
[20] Bryant, p. 176.

Antony. Indeed, his analysis often proves more limiting than unifying. The first lines of the play remind us of this past, of

> his goodly eyes
> That o'er the files and musters of the war
> Have glow'd like plated Mars,
>
> (I, i, 2-4)

and of

> his captain's heart,
> Which in the scuffles of great fights hath burst
> The buckles on his breast.
>
> (I, i, 6-8)

The magnitude of the Emperor Antony, then, must be judged as it interacts not only with Antony's literal or "real" size, but with his "diminution" (III, xiii, 198) in the eyes of the Roman mob, and also with the stature of his past soldiership. Thus, in the single scene alone we must contrast the "plated Mars", with the bellows to cool a gypsy's lust, with the actor who enters as Antony on the stage, and finally with the Antony created by Cleopatra's love (V, ii). No single image of Antony, moreover (contrary to the assertion of some critics), is the Antony advocated by either Shakespeare or the play. The Antony of the play may be glimpsed only in the perpetual and dramatic interaction of the images within the world of the play itself.

Those who have often selected one of these visions of Antony as the "true" image of the play, have presented equally convincing evidence of "mutually exclusive" views. Utilizing the same world imagery as Miss Spurgeon and Miss Pogson as evidence for his thesis, Nicoll contends that the cosmic images seem "at least to a certain extent, forced and imposed rather than integrated with the central theme".[21] William Rosen is even more complete in his denunciation of the colossal stature viewed by Miss Spurgeon and Miss Pogson:

No matter how grandiose the imagery of Antony's speeches in this scene [I, i], to extract an imagery pattern stressing the colossal nature of love, to say that Shakespeare here magnifies Antony's figure and

[21]   Nicoll, p. 152.

presents his love as life's highest value, is to neglect dramatic situation and indulge in romantic delusion.[22]

In his effort to consider this "dramatic situation" Rosen notes that "it is important to view the words of Philo and Antony as part of the dramatic context of the scene". "The meaning of the play", he says with an assurance that his subject should be singular,[23] "cannot be said to derive wholly from what the hero says of himself." [24] "When Antony and Cleopatra come on stage", he continues, "the audience has been prepared to view them as they appear to the world, and their words do not contradict that view." [25] While Rosen has rightly directed our attention toward the dramatic interaction of Philo's description of Antony with the hero's own actions and words, we must surely take issue with his conclusion that these words "do not contradict that view". While Demetrius in the scene agrees with Rosen that Antony "approaches the common liar, who/ Thus speaks of him at Rome" (ll. 60-61), we as audience do not. Philo's advice to "behold and see" (l. 13) includes not only the meeting of Antony and Cleopatra here, but their other meetings as well. Although we may or may not agree with Demetrius in terms of what we see and hear in this scene, we surely do not in terms of all that we see and hear by the end of the play. If Demetrius, like the equally Reasonable Theseus, might well exclaim, "The lover, all as frantic,/ Sees Helen's beauty in a brow of Egypt" [26] (A Midsummer-Night's Dream, V, i, 10-11), the audience by the end of the play would surely reply in Hippolyta's words that their love playing "grows to something of great constancy;/ But, howsoever, strange and admirable" (ll. 26-27). Indeed, we might argue that the whole

[22] Rosen, p. 110.
[23] See question structure, Chapter V.
[24] Rosen, p. 110.
[25] Ibid., pp. 110-111.
[26] The idea that Cleopatra as an Egyptian or "gypsy" was universally considered unattractive by Elizabethans has often been footnoted by lines from Shakespeare out of context. If all of Mercutio's speech and the tone with which it is delivered are taken into account, Cleopatra's beauty is acknowledged (Romeo and Juliet, II, iv, 38-48). Robert Burton also acknowledges her beauty, in The Anatomy of Melancholy, edited Rev. A. R. Shilleto (London, G. Bell and Sons, 1916), III, 179.

movement of the play is from infinite variety and chance to that event which shackles accident and bolts up change.[27] If we doubt the sincerity of the lovers' hyperbole in the first scene, Middleton Murry explains that "their acts gradually, and reluctantly, move into harmony with their utterance; and, as the acts slowly change their nature, so the quality of the utterance becomes more rich and rare."[28] Elias Schwartz, echoes the idea that while the protagonists speak "the language, not of lovers, but of parodists of love", there is, nonetheless, "a kind of before hand irony in the conceits, for they will later assume real validity".[29]

With his usual perception Maynard Mack studies "Shakespeare's duality of attitude toward his lovers".[30] He regards *Antony and Cleopatra* both as Shakespeare's *Paradiso*,[31] and yet a play in which the infernal tone reflects the "ultimately destructive character of their relationship".[32] Mirroring still another view of the tone of the world imagery, then, Mack speaks of the "ambiguity"[33] of the play that assigns its lovers neither to Paradise nor to the Inferno. "Shakespeare", he proposes, "holds the balance even, and does not decide for us who finally is the strumpet of the play, Antony's Cleopatra, or Caesar's Fortune, and who, therefore, is the 'strumpet's fool'."[34] While the play's ambiguity argues for the dramatic presentation of a number of sides of a philosophical question,[35] the play as a whole surely proposes a kind of implied answer to its rhetorical questions. By the end of the play, our dramatic sympathy makes evident that Caesar's Fortune, not Antony's Cleopatra, is more the strumpet

[27] See discussion of love and Fortune, Chapter IV, and progression from infinite variety to that which shackles accidents and bolts up change in the love-act structure, Chapter V.

[28] John Middleton Murry, *Shakespeare* (London, Jonathan Cape, 1936), p. 378.

[29] Elias Schwartz, "The Shackling of Accidents: *Antony and Cleopatra*", *College English*, XXIII (April, 1962), 551.

[30] Maynard Mack, p. 16.

[31] *Ibid.*, p. 15.

[32] *Ibid.*, p. 20.

[33] *Ibid.*, p. 21.

[34] *Ibid.*, p. 23.

[35] See discussion of question structure, Chapter IV.

of the play.[36] Thus, while Mack's study is characteristically penetrating, it is also necessarily limited by its very brevity.[37]

If G. Wilson Knight too often sacrifices theme to tone and
rhapsodic appreciation, his study remains not only the most ambitious, but the most penetrating of the studies of the play. In
this single sustained study of the imagery of *Antony and Cleopatra*, Knight, in such critical observations as "all evil, however,
is resolved, in the whole",[38] ultimately aligns himself with those
who view the play as totally idealistc. Knight would view the play,
then, as Enobarbus views Cleopatra, as making "defect perfection" (II, ii, 231). That defect, however, rather than being resolved into perfection, remains an integral part of the total vision
of the play. Knight, nonetheless, is keenly aware of the "realistic,
and, indeed, coarse essences" [39] of the play, even if they are
"resolved" in the "ascending scale" of the play. "The style", he
explains, "the poetic vision of the whole, endorses this movement:
it views its world as one rising from matter to spirit . . .".[40] Not
only does Knight catalogue the many images of "melting", "dis-
solving", "mingling", and "mating",[41] but he interprets them
thematically as well: "For the blending of elements is similar to
the blending of the sexes in love which is our main story: and
from that we pass, even farther, to a blending of life and death." [42]
Knight's belief in the utter resolution of the coarse elements of
the play in the whole becomes immediately apparent in the title
of his chapter on the play, "The Transcendental Humanism of
Antony and Cleopatra".

---

[36] See discussion of dramatic sympathy, Chapter II.
[37] His introduction runs from pages 15 to 23 in The Penguin Paperback
edition of the play.
[38] Knight, p. 199.
[39] *Ibid.*
[40] *Ibid.*, pp. 204-205.
[41] *Ibid.*, pp. 218-227.
[42] *Ibid.*, p. 236. Aristophanes' discussion of the legend of the division of
the sexes by the gods and the search for union with "the other half" in
Plato's *Symposium* has often been pointed to as a parallel, but no possibility that Shakespeare could have read the *Symposium* has been raised.
MacCallum, for example, points to the parallel and finds it "surprising"
(pp. 445-447).

Utilizing the same imperative, "Let Rome in Tiber melt" (I, i, 33), that Knight points to as an illustration [43] of "the blending of the sexes in love", Holloway argues for a clearly opposing view of the tone of the play. He sees the line instead as an example of "Antony's curse on the world of his public life", and remarks further that "Antony and Cleopatra both estrange themselves from the environment they grandiosely dominate." [44] He parallels Antony's curse with Cleopatra's orders:

> Give me ink and paper
> He shall have every day a several greeting,
> Or *I'll unpeople Egypt.*
>
> (I, v, 76-78)

Although Holloway admits that the italics are his, he points to an intended emphasis in the lines by commenting that they "have a special prominence at the end of Act I." [45] Aside from my differing view of the lines analyzed *in context* [46] (the italics are mine), the Act divisions are those of later editors, and in any case would pass unnoticed in a continuous Elizabethan production. The first Folio has no act and scene divisions except "*Actus Primus. Scaena Prima*". An analysis of "Antony's curse" in context shows Holloway's position as unsound as that of the supposed "malediction" of Cleopatra's orders. In the context of the first scene of the play Antony's lines surely have out dramatic sympathy. After all, it is to Cleopatra that Antony speaks when he says,

> Let Rome in Tiber melt, and the wide arch
> Of the rang'd empire fall! Here is my space,
> Kingdoms are clay: our dungy earth alike
> Feeds beast as man; the nobleness of life
> Is to do thus: when such a mutual pair,
> And such a train can do't, in which I bind,
> On pain of punishment, the world to weet
> We stand up peerless.
>
> (I, i, 33-40)

Antony's exaggeration is not so much a "curse" as the hyperbole

---

[43]   *Ibid.*, p. 235.
[44]   Holloway, p. 113.
[45]   *Ibid.*
[46]   See discussion, Chapter II.

proper to lovers.[47] We would have him promise no less. Surely at this point in the play, we would not have him choose Fulvia rather than Cleopatra. We neither care nor are prodded to care to meet Fulvia, and would have him meet often with the cloyless Cleopatra.

In contrast to Knight's description of "ascending scale", John F. Danby's view of the movement of the play begins with Knight's blending of the sexes and moves toward Holloway's view of estrangement. He sees in *Antony and Cleopatra* "the opposites that merge, unite and fall apart".[48] Aligning himself, however, more with Mack than with Holloway, Danby speaks of "ambiguity" as "central to Shakespeare's experience [?] in the play." [49] Although he observes that "if it is wrong to see the 'mutual pair' as a strumpet and her fool, it is also wrong to see them as a Phoenix and a Turtle",[50] he sounds more like Holloway than Mack in his description of "the self-destruction of things that rot with the motion which their own nature and situation dictate".[51] His stated stance of ambiguity virtually disappears when he speaks of this self-destructive focus as "almost obsessive with Shakespeare throughout the play".[52] There is no hint of Knight's ascending scale. "The fourth and fifth acts of *Antony and Cleopatra* are not epiphanies", he explains, but

the ends moved to by that process whereby things rot themselves with motion – unhappy and bedizened and sordid, streaked with the mean, the ignoble, the contemptible. Shakespeare may have his plays in which "redemption" is a theme (and I think he has), but *Antony and Cleopatra* is not one of them.[53]

When Shaw, like Danby,[54] explains that "the very name of Cleopatra suggests at once a tragedy of Circe," [55] we have a proposal

---

47   See discussion of the limitlessness of love, Chapter IV.
48   Danby, p. 140.
49   *Ibid.*, p. 130.
50   *Ibid.*
51   *Ibid.*, p. 140.
52   *Ibid.*, p. 141.
53   *Ibid.*, p. 148.
54   *Ibid.*, p. 145.
55   Shaw, p. xxviii.

of a tone very different from that of a *Paradise* – indeed, like
Traversi in his picture of the differing views of characterization,
we might well conclude that the views are more "mutually exclusive" than "ambiguous".

Perhaps the most recent attempts, however, to solve the problem of the mutually exclusive interpretations of images such as
the world images have been by proposing a satiric quality in their
readings. Thus, in this view, the dominating tone of the world
images is neither purely holy nor completely degrading. Often,
nonetheless, this comic note, once noticed, is itself seen as a
blemish in the play. Mark Van Doren, for example, notes of the
hero and heroine: "They would seem to have been cut out for
comedy and indeed there is much comedy here. Only a supreme
effort at writing keeps the play on its tragic keel." [56] The pejorative implications here echo those who speak of the tone of corruption. Comedy is clearly viewed as an inferior genre. While the
possible profundity of comedy has been underestimated from the
very beginnings of literary criticism, many of man's deepest
thoughts have repeatedly been expressed in his comic literature.
Meredith in *An Essay on Comedy* might well be speaking of
those who have commented pejoratively on the comedy in *Antony
and Cleopatra* when he says that "people are ready to surrender
themselves to witty thumps on the back, breast, and sides; all
except the head – and it is there it aims".[57]

He explains further that "there are plain reasons why the comic
poet remains without a fellow. A society of cultivated men and
women is required, wherein ideas are current, and the perceptions
quick, that he may be supplied with matter and an audience." [58]
Here, then, is the crux of the problem, the reason that the comedy
in the play has been viewed solely as a flaw: comedy is intellectual
because it requires a background or standard with which to compare the ridiculous, for one of the bases of comedy (indeed, of

---

[56] Mark Van Doren, *Shakespeare* (Garden City, New York, Doubleday,
1939), p. 239.
[57] George Meredith, *An Essay on Comedy and the Uses of the Comic
Spirit*, ed. Lane Cooper (Ithaca, New York, Cornell University Press,
1956), p. 76.
[58] *Ibid.*, p. 75.

drama) is contrast and incongruity (and many of the critics have lacked that background). Shakespeare hardly lacked a cultivated Elizabethan audience to appreciate the comedy of *Antony and Cleopatra*.[59] He seems to have wanted such a cultivated critical audience since then. Yet the observation in *Paradise Lost* that "smiles from Reason flow" [60] is one to which Renaissance plays and critics pay tribute.[61] Indeed, the idea that *"this world is a comedy to those who think, a tragedy to those who feel"* [62] was not yet lost to some in the eigtheenth century. That contrast and incongruity (concepts obviously more thematic than that of mere "comic relief") form the basis of comedy was evident to Sidney, who observed that "laughter almost ever cometh of things most disproportioned to ourselves and nature",[63] and to Castiglione, who stated yet more dogmatically that "we laugh only at those

---

[59] For the view that Shakespeare's audience was composed of more than ignorant groundlings, see Alfred Harbage, *Shakespeare's Audience* (New York, Columbia University Press, 1941).

[60] Milton, *Paradise Lost*, IX, 239.

[61] Jonson, prologue to "Volpone" in *Works* (ll. 20-22):
"no egges are broken;
Nor quaking custards with fierce teeth affrighted,
Wherewith your rout are so delighted."
Cf. Francis Beaumont and John Fletcher, "The Knight of the Burning Pestle", in *Works*, ed. A. R. Waller (Cambridge, University Press, 1908), VI, 60 (prologue): Our "intent was ... to move inward delight, not outward lightness; and to breed (if it might be) soft smiling, not loud laughing: knowing it (to the wise) to be a great pleasure, to hear Counsel mixed with Wit, as to the foolish to have sport mingled with rudeness."
Sidney, pp. 451-452: "But our comedians think there is no delight without laughter; which is very wrong, for though laughter may come with delight, yet cometh it not of delight, as though delight should be the cause of laughter; but well may one thing breed both together. Nay rather in themselves they have, as it were, a kind of contrariety; for delight we scarecely do but in things that have a conveniency to ourselves or to the general nature; laughter almost ever cometh of things most disproportioned to ourselves and nature. Delight hath a joy in it, either permanent or present. Laughter hath only a scornful tickling. For example, we are ravished with delight to see a fair woman, and yet are far from being moved to laughter. We can laugh at deformed creatures, wherein certainly we cannot delight."

[62] Horace Walpole, "Letter to Sir Horace Mann" (31 December 1769) in *Letters*, ed. Peter Cunningham (London, Richard Bentley and Son, 1891), V, 212.

[63] Sidney, p. 452.

things that have incongruity in them".[64] Baudelaire suggests these elements of contrast and incongruity as the very essence of laughter:

Le rire est satanique il est donc profondément humain. Il est dans l'homme la conséquence de l'idée de sa propre supériorité; et, en effet, comme le rire est essentiellement humain, il est essentiellement contradictoire, c'est-à-dire qu'il est à la fois signe d'une grandeur infinie et d'une misère infinie, misère infinie relativement à l'Etre absolu dont il possède la conception, grandeur infinie relativement aux animaux.[65]

Suggestions of comedy in the play, however, like suggestions of grandeur and decay have been offered purely as tone. Other functions of the comedy have been ignored, except for the ubiquitous catch-all, comic relief. That the comedy makes a serious comment in the themes of the play has never been demonstrated. Showing more an appreciation of the comedy than an analysis, Brents Stirling observes that

a "satirical tragedy" like *Antony and Cleopatra* is in no sense anomalous. Although spirited it is soberly honest; although astringent it is sympathetic; and although realistic in outlook it contains great art. *It* has the stature, whether or not the hero attains greatness, and it, not Antony or Cleopatra, embodies the ultimate insight intended for an audience. *Antony and Cleopatra* asserts human dignity, value, because it confronts defeat with a superb expression of ironical truth.[66]

Like comments concerning its tone, moreover, comments about the play's meanings have been both narrow and vague. The play is seen as having a single meaning, an "ultimate insight", to match its single, dominating tone. Those who view the play's corruption, view the play as totally negative in its approach toward love; those who view its comedy often terms its approach completely affirmative. Thus, for example, Daniel Pollack notes that "the play has a very definite tragic side, but the total effect is one of

[64] Baldassare Castiglione, *The Book of the Courtier*, trans. Sir Thomas Hoby (New York, E. P. Dutton, 1956), p. 138.
[65] Charles Baudelaire, "De L'essence du Rire et Généralement du Comique dans les Arts Plastiques", in *Œuvres Complètes*, ed. F. F. Gautier (Paris, Nouvelle Revue Française, 1925), V, 344.
[66] Brents Stirling, p. 191.

comic affirmation rather than tragic negation".[67] "It seems to me", he continues, "that irony is precisely the literary device which Shakespeare uses to achieve this sense of affirmation." [68] Rare indeed is the analysis of a particular comic passage or its role in the themes of the play. Schwartz, as we have seen, does comment specifically on the opening lines of Antony and Cleopatra. He notes that their language, a parody of the language of lovers, later assumes "a real validity".[69] But he fails to mention any thematic or structural implications of this fact. Bradley also notes the "amusing" nature of the first half of the play, but sees it only as a flaw in the tragedy.[70] Yet surely the progression from parody to validity is a part of Knight's ascending scale. Indeed, the play does move from the parody of love (from the "love game" [71]) to a "more valid" love. The repeated ritual of "the art of love", then, may be viewed as the lowest, but nonetheless essential, rung of the play's ladder of love.

Miss Maizitis in another of those rare analyses of the comic nature of a specific passage comments on II, vii, 40-50:

Lep. What manner o' thing is your crocodile?
Ant. It is shap'd, sir, like itself, and it is as it is, and moves with its own organs. It lives by that which nourisheth it, and the elements once out of it, it transmigrates.
Lep. What colour is it of?
Ant. Of it own colour too.
Lep. 'Tis a strange serpent.
Ant. 'Tis so, and the tears of it are wet.
Caes. Will this description satisfy him?

Miss Maizitis observes that the lines are "a parody of the reasonable way of life, the life for which Caesar stands and against which Antony and Cleopatra revolt: and Caesar is himself forced to comment on the inadequacy of it when he inquires, 'Will this

---

[67]   Daniel Arthur Pollack, "Again for Cydnus: An Essay on the Comic Irony of Shakespeare's Antony and Cleopatra" (Unpublished Honors Thesis, Harvard College, 1960), p. i.
[68]   Ibid.
[69]   See footnote 29, p. 69 above.
[70]   Bradley, Oxford Lectures, pp. 284-285.
[71]   See David L. Stevenson, The Love-Game Comedy (New York, Columbia University Press, 1946).

satisfy him?' " [72] Beyond the unpublished remark of Miss Maizitis, the passage is referred to only as an example of comic relief or of Cleopatra as crocodile.[73] Charney mentions only line 38: "This mouthful of sibilants is almost too much for the tipsy Lepidus." [74] Otherwise the thematic implications of the passage have been ignored.[75] Yet the very length and questioning tone of the passage argues for a more thematic interpretation.[76] The sexual nature of Antony's speech that immediately precedes his discussion with Lepidus (ll. 17-23) directs our interpretation of that discussion.

The comic tone pervades even the colossal imagery that we have noted and has thematic significance there as well. When, for example, Cleopatra ironically alludes to the stature of Antony's past soldiership in order to hold him, the world images are seen to take on a fuller and more varied role in the themes of the play. Thus when Cleopatra says,

> They are so still,
> Or thou, the greatest soldier of the world,
> Art turn'd the greatest liar,
>
> (I, iii, 37-39)

the stature of Antony's past, present, and future all dramatically interact. There is more than the building of tragic stature in the colossal images of Hercules. When the comic overtones of her chiding statement, "This Herculean Roman does become/ The carriage of his chafe" (I, iii, 84-85), are realized, we see in the coquettish mockery, Antony's past glory, his present diminution, and even the foreshadowing of the Emperor Antony. Likewise when the soldier suggests that Antony desist from fighting by sea (III, vii, 60) and declares "By Hercules I think I am i' the right", the expletive does more than inform us (like North's Plutarch) [77]

---

[72] Maizitis, pp. 168-169.

[73] See, for example, Daniel Stempel, "The Transmigration of the Crocodile", *Shakespeare Quarterly*, VII (1956), 59-72.

[74] Charney, p. 97.

[75] The passage is completely ignored thematically in both the New Arden and the Variorum editions of the play.

[76] See comparison of "strange serpent" with "odd worm" of the Clown episode (V, ii) above, and discussion of both love and reason and love and mystery, Chapter IV.

[77] Plutarch, II, 6.

that Antony is descended from Anton, the son of Hercules. It serves the dramatic purpose of foreshadowing the god's leaving of Antony (IV, iii, 15-16) and compares and contrasts the man with the god. We cannot, then, comment on any isolated single effect of the comedy any more than we can comment on the isolated single effect of a given image or cluster of images.

Rather than a flaw or comic relief, we suggest that the roles of the comic passages are both integral and manifold. Comedy functions in the imagery, themes, structure, and charactrizations in the play. Thus, the comic tone directs the interpretation of the imagery, contrasts the comic servants with the protagonists,[78] dramatizes the love play of the lovers in the love-act structure,[79] and thematically presents the ridiculous [80] that is as much a part of "this Tragicomedy of love [81] as is the sublime. "To laugh" is as much a part of the infinite variety of the art and nature of love as "to chide" or "to weep" (I, i, 49-50). The art of laughing in love prevents cloying. It forms that part of the "heavenly mingle" (I, v, 59) that prevents the sublime from overpowering all else. It is present in Cleopatra's very first dialogue with Antony and extends not only to Antony's death scene (e.g., IV, xv, 32 and 59) but also to her own (V, ii, 300-307). Indeed, the comedy also dramatizes the complementary nature of lovers, for when Antony weeps, Cleopatra is mirthful; when he is laughing, she is sullen sick (I, iii, 3-5). No Diotima or Ovid need tell Cleopatra that opposites attract.[82]

A major portion of the comedy (as with so much of our comic literature) is concerned with bawdry. Although no adequate analysis of the relation between laughter and sex has ever been given, we may find a hint to the answer in the contrast between the rational part of man which aspires to the angelic and his animal appetites. This is the contradiction to which Baudelaire alludes above. Perhaps the most concise insight into the relationship be-

[78] See the discussion of the comic levels in *Romeo and Juliet* and *Antony and Cleopatra*, Chapter II.
[79] See discussion, Chapter V.
[80] See discussion of Antony and Cleopatra as "fools", Chapter II.
[81] Burton, III, 217.
[82] See discussion of the attraction of opposites, Chapter IV.

tween sexual bawdry and laughter is seen in a single line in *Paradise Lost*: "Thy mate, who sees when thou art seen least wise." [83] Puttenham sees a clear kinship between bawdry and comedy. When he speaks of those "things that moue a man to laughter", he explains that "it is for some vndecencie that is foūd in them: which maketh it decent for euery man to laugh at them".[94] Castelvetro also notes that some of the "pleasing things that move us to laughter are all the things that pertain to carnal delight, as the secret part of the body, lascivious connections, memories of them, and things that are like them".[85] Surely, then, any play that attempts to dramatize with any fullness the nature of love must include the comedy of "carnal delight".

Yet justifications for the bawdry have seemed as necessary to some recent critics [86] as those for the comedy. The best defense, if any be necessary, are those of the Renaissance critics and poets themselves. In a discussion that justifies Cleopatra's bawdy wit as much as the bawdry of the play, Castiglione suggests that a

woman ought not therefore (to make her selfe good and honest) be so squeimish and make wise to abhorre both the company and the talke (though somewhat of the wantonest) if she bee present, to get her thence by and by, for a man may lightly gesse that she fained to be so coye to hide that in her selfe which she doubted others might come to the knowledge of: and such nice fashions are alwaies hateful.[87]

Sidney in his discussion of comedy decorously argues that he "who seeth not the filthiness of evil wanteth a great foil to perceive the beauty of virtue".[88] If Sidney stresses the *utile* of bawdry, Puttenham emphasizes its *dulce*: "Vicious manners of speech [are] sometimes and some cases tollerable, and chiefly

---

[83] Milton, *Paradise Lost*, VIII, 578.
[84] Puttenham, p. 291.
[85] Lodovico Castelvetro, *On the Poetics*, trans. Allan H. Gilbert in *Literary Criticism*, p. 314.
[86] See, for example, Edward Hubler, *The Sense of Shakespeare's Sonnets* (New York, Hill and Wang, 1952), p. 50.
   Cf. Partridge, p. 6.
[87] Castiglione, p. 191.
[88] Sidney, p. 432.

to the intent to mooue laughter, and to make sport...".[89]

Many have seen the bawdy comedy as degrading; others, from ignorance or a false sense of decorum, have simply ignored it. Some have even denied its existence. Although Granville-Barker sees the play as one "dominated by sexual passion",[90] others have seen its spacious idealism as unmarred by passion. H. H. Furness, for example, gallantly defends the play against charges of bawdry simply by refusing to notice any:

> Where is there any scene of passion? Where is there a word which, had it been addressed by a husband to a wife, we should not approve? ... Is wandering through the streets and noting the quality of the people sensual? Is fishing sensual? Is teasing past endurance sensual?[91]

The questions themselves are comic. While his second question strongly implies that marriage excludes passion, his last is even more absurd once we realize the sensual purpose of Cleopatra's teasing. Surely it is a part of the love game, the love play that excites. Furness' naiveté concerning the fishing images is as complete as that of Miss Maizitis, who also dismisses any analysis with the simple "critical" description of the protagonists, who, "of all things go fishing".[92] Indeed, the tone of the passage in context is so sensual that we need only point to II, v, 9 ff. to explain the overtones of "he fishes" in I, iv, 4. No knowledge of Freud is necessary to understand the sexual connotations of either fishing or horseback riding (I, v, 19 ff.; Cf. III, vii, 7 ff.; III, x, 10). The relationship between riding a horse and sexual intercourse which Freud describes was known to Ovid[93] as well as to Burton.[94] Indeed, it was a relationship seen in North's translation of "The Life of Marcus Antonius".[95] Shakespeare himself with

[89] Puttenham, p. 253.
[90] Granville-Barker, "Prefaces to Shakespeare", p. 125.
[91] Furness, Variorum edition of *Antony and Cleopatra*, p. xiv.
[92] Maizitis, p. 199.
[93] Ovid, "The Loves", in *"The Loves"*, *"The Art of Beauty"*, *"The Remedies for Love"*, and *"The Art of Love"*, trans. Rolfe Humphries (Bloomington, Indiana University Press, 1957), II, 1-17.
[94] Burton, III, 194.
[95] Plutarch, II, 55.

less than subtle passion utilizes the analogy in his early *Venus and Adonis*:

> Now is she in the very lists of love,
> Her champion mounted for the hot encounter:
> All is imaginary she doth prove,
> He will not manage her, although he mount her;
> That worse than Tantalus' is her annoy,
> To clip Elysium, and to lack her joy.
>
> (ll. 595-600)

The fishing images in *Antony and Cleopatra*, such as II, v, 9 ff., are as self-explanatory as "Groping for trouts in a peculiar stream" is in the context of *Measure for Measure* (I, ii, 91). These images demonstrate the sexual basis of love and not, as Miss Spurgeon would have it, that his "fishing similes" are "ordinary", and therefore that they show "no sign of personal knowledge or interest" [96] on Shakespeare's part.

Even Eric Partridge, who tells us in the very title of his famous study that Shakespeare is bawdy, declines to impart any relevance to that fact. He merely notes (with the biographical slant of Miss Spurgeon) that *Antony and Cleopatra* was written in a period in which Shakespeare "suffered from sex-nausea".[97] Even an intuitive feeling of the spaciousness and corruption of the play is more reflective of the play and more enlightening than such a "study". Yet Partridge himself does intuitively note that "in my study of Shakespeare's sexuality and bawdiness, I have come to feel that, from his plays and poems, there emerges something basic, significant, supremely important and most illuminatingly revelatory".[98] In spite of the vigor of the series, the thought remains intuitively stagnant rather than analytically suggestive. Virtually the only other study which demonstrates a recognition of the sexual images without viewing them as totally disgusting is that of Charney, but the end of his study is tone and characterization. Like comedy in general, the possible profundity of comic bawdry has long been ignored. "To these I will giue none other aunswere",

---

[96] Spurgeon, p. 31.
[97] Partridge, p. 52.
[98] *Ibid.*, pp. 55-56.

Puttenham flatly retorts, "then referre them to the many trifling poems of *Homer, Ouid, Virgill, Catullus* and other notable writers of former ages, which were not of any grauitie or seriousnesse, and many of them full of impudicitie and ribaudrie . . .".[99] Indeed, of his own work Shakespeare might well have admitted, like Puttenham, that he could "not denie but these conceits of mine be trifles: no lesse in very deede be all the most serious studies of man . . .".[100]

While little meaning has been seen in even the most serious sections of what the critics have termed a marvelous, spacious, sensual, but ultimately only dazzling play, less has been seen in the sexual bawdry. Even Charney, for example, who notes the phallic nature of the sword images in the play, neglects the equally phallic overtones of the serpent images. Yet Charney's study of the serpent cluster probes far deeper than Daniel Stempfel's, which, of course, proposes that the cluster stems "directly from Renaissance misogyny" and "are all associated with Cleopatra".[101] The images, he tells us, "fall into three classes: references to magic and witchcraft, to poisons, and to serpents", and explains further "that these are actually a single group united by the common theme of witchcraft in its broadest (and worst) connotations".[102] Indeed, most critics who have remarked on the serpent images have noted chiefly their satanic qualities. These critics regard the play in much the same way Brandes did: "Everything sank, everything fell – character and will, dominions and principalities, men and women. Everything was worm-eaten, serpent-bitten, poisoned by sensuality – everything tottered and collapsed." [103] Cleopatra, then, in this view, becomes "as we all know her, the woman of women, quintessentiated Eve, or rather Eve and the serpent in one – 'My serpent of the Old Nile,' as Antony calls her".[104] To support his contention that this is the

---

[99]   Puttenham, p. 111.
[100]   *Ibid.*, p. 112.
[101]   Stempel, p. 66.
[102]   *Ibid.*
[103]   Brandes, p. 462.
[104]   *Ibid.* (More precisely, this is the way Cleopatra recalls that Antony addresses her.)

primary purpose of the serpent-image cluster, he notes "that in moments of angry emotion Cleopatra envisions the Nile with its vipers".[105] The same tone is still evident in the recent comment of J. W. Lever:

Cleopatra's own Egypt is a fallen country infested with serpents; the snake is never far from her thoughts, until the time comes for her to die of its sting. In this lost paradise her wooing of Antony is comic and sensual, immoral and thoroughly reprehensible. Shakespeare's vision, however, miraculously transcends all this with its perspective of a paradise regained in the union of love and death. Through the fiery consummation of that union, the mortal lovers become immortals: in no world of nature nor in a spiritual heaven, but in another un-known country of the imagination.[106]

Again we notice the characteristically pejorative view of the comic and the sensual, and how "Shakespeare's vision" miraculously "transcends" both these "reprehensible" qualities.

Even Charney, who comments more fully on the sexual imagery in the play than anyone else, mentions the serpent imagery only as a blemish. Phallic overtones are neglected. Of the Clown episode in V, ii, he notes only that "his speech in this scene is full of overtones of Eve and the serpent, which comic asides on man's mortality, and it raises the serpent theme to an important symbolic level".[107] He regards the episode as "a fine bit of comic relief",[108] and having made clear his awareness of comedy assumes that no serious themes are dramatized. Thus, while the serpent images may have "an important symbolic level", the presence of comedy excludes any serious analysis here, it seems. Although Charney mentions that in this episode "the serpent now sym-bolizes the love-making of death",[109] Partridge does not even include either "serpent" or "worm" in his "comprehensive" glos-sary. Yet the "strange serpent" of II, vii, 24 and 48 is surely as sexually significant as the "odd worm" of V, ii, 257, to which it is obviously to be compared. The sexual connotations of the worm in the play, though often obvious, have rarely, if ever, been

[105] Clemen, p. 160.
[106] Lever, p. 87.
[107] Charney, p. 100.
[108] *Ibid.*
[109] *Ibid.*, p. 101.

commented upon. Yet the worm is emphasized as being "pretty" (l. 243) and filled with "joy" (ll. 259 and 278). The sexual pun on dying (so common in Elizabethan literature) is common in the play. Although critics have pointed to the pun in Antony's famous "I am dying, Egypt, dying" (IV, xv, 18 and 41), they have not sufficiently noted the sexual connotations of the worms that "kills and pains not" (l. 243). Yet the pun occurs and recurs throughout the passage. We hear that "those that do die of it, do seldom or never recover" (ll. 246-247). The very choice of the word "desire" for example, makes the connotations clear to the careful modern reader as well as to a member of the Elizabethan audience: "but I would not be the part that should desire you to touch him, for his biting is immortal" (ll. 244-245). Indeed, the word "immortal" here reflects the same longing for immortality in the sexual desire as seen in Plato's *Symposium* on love as well as in Shakespeare's own Sonnets. Such a sexual reading is necessary to understand not only the puns on "dying", but on "lying" (cf. Sonnet 138 in which the pun is belabored) and "honesty" (cf. *Othello*, for example). The Clown, then, tells us not only that "Very many, men and women" have died "on't", but that

I heard of one of them no longer than yesterday, a very honest woman, but something give to lie, as a woman should not do, but in the way of honesty, how she died of the biting of it, what pain she felt: truly, she makes a very good report o' the worm: but he that will believe all that they say, shall never be saved by half that they do: but this is most falliable, the worm's an odd worm.
(ll. 249-257)

In fact the passage is so much richer with the sexual level added to the literal level of death and the asp that it would be prideful to assume that the reading was our own and not Shakespeare's "intention". We can agree that by this point in our consideration of love in the play the worm of love is truly "a strange serpent", "an odd worm" as mysterious and incommunicable as Cleopatra's attempts to describe it in I, iii, 88 f. Yet, if mysterious,[110] love is also as self-explanatory as Antony's explanations of the serpent to Lepidus: that is, it is "Of it own colour" (II, vii, 47), "lives by

[110]   See discussion of the mystery of love, Chapter IV.

that which nourisheth it" (ll. 43-44; cf. Sonnet 73), and "the elements once out of it", it transmigrates" (ll. 44-45).

Still the sexual nature of the Clown's speech is continually ignored. While it is the naturalness of the sexual act (a major theme in *Measure for Measure*) that is emphasized in "the worm will do its kind" (V, ii, 261-262), for example, the line is repeatedly and literally glossed solely as "the worm will do 'what his nature dictates' ".[111] In addition to the puns on "dying", "lying", and "honesty", there are lines that are not only richer with a sexual reading, but have little other meaning: "Look you, the worm is not to be trusted, but in the keeping of wise people: for indeed, there is no goodness in the worm" (ll. 264-266). The sexual connotations, moreover, are continued and related to the food-imagery cluster as Cleopatra asks, "Will it eat me?" (l. 270) and the clown replies:

You must not think I am so simple but I know the devil himself will not eat a woman: I know that a woman is a dish for the gods, if the devil dress her not. But truly these same whoreson devils do the gods great harm in their women: for in every ten that they make, the devils mar five.

(ll. 271-276)

The sexual overtones are clear in "dress", "whoreson", "make", and "mar", as well as in the food imagery of "dish" and "eat". When Cleopatra says, "Have I the aspic in my lips" (l. 292), Charney observes that "this passage shows Cleopatra as the 'serpent of the old Nile' again" and that "Cleopatra's 'Immortal longings' recall the Clown's caution that the biting of the asp is immortal".[112] Still he neglects to draw the more revealing similarity between the worm that "kills and pains not" and "The stroke of death" that "is as a lover's pinch,/ Which hurts and is desir'd" (ll. 294-295). Surely the word "desir'd" here again directs us to the combined pleasure and pain of the sexual act.

These "coarse" and "realistic" elements in the play are not, as we have seen, "resolved in the whole" or lost in the "ascending scale" of the play as Knight suggests, but are merely transmuted

---

[111] V, ii, 261-262n.
[112] Charney, p. 100.

into the higher. Thus even as Cleopatra says, "I am fire, and air; my other elements/ I give to baser life" (ll. 288-289), the baser elements of the earth and water of the Nile (both "fruitful and lethal") [113] are indirectly called to mind. Even in the fire and air, then, we are reminded of the "strange serpent" that "lives by that which nourisheth it, and the elements once out of it, it trans-migrates" (II, vii, 43-48). Cleopatra, refusing the dungy earth of the beggar and Caesar alike (V, ii, 7-8), no longer depends upon either food or Fortune as she becomes fire and air. This distaste of "our dungy earth" (I, i, 35 ff.), moreover, is one she and Antony have felt from the very first scene of the play. But in the ascending scale, the two baser [114] elements, water and earth (the "fertile ooze" that Charney discusses so well) [115] are not dis-missed; they are as much a part of "Shakespeare's vision" in the play as the fire and air into which they are transmuted. The bawdry of the play is the foundation, the bottom rung of its ladder of love, upon which the spiritual love is built and upon which it depends for support.

The food imagery, to which we have alluded in passing, has also been considered as functioning almost solely as tone. Just as the serpent images have been viewed as sprinkled capriciously over the play to add a touch of corruption and the world images to add a dash of stature, so have the food or banquet images been seen as creating a sensual atmosphere for the play. When the food images have been noticed and catalogued, they have been analyzed as they shed light only on tone, characterization, or Shakespeare's personal food tastes. [116] Rarely have their thematic implications been explored. Clemen, moreover, when he char-acterizes Cleopatra "on the lowest level" as "a morsel to be coveted", [117] speaks not of the multiple effects of the food imagery

[113] *Ibid.*, p. 101.
[114] For a full discussion of the order of the elements, see Leone Ebreo (Leo Hebraeus), *The Philosophy of Love (Dialoghi d'Amore)*, trans. F. Friedeberg-Sieley and Jean H. Barnes (London, The Soncino Press, 1937), pp. 78-89.
[115] Charney, pp. 96 ff.
[116] See, for example, Spurgeon, pp. 320-321; Clemen, p. 167; Charney, pp. 102-107; and Knight, pp. 219 ff.
[117] Clemen, p. 167.

or even of a specific image in context. Again the equation between the sensual and the pejorative is seen in his phrase, "On
the lowest level". Even the euphemistic "coveted" for "eaten"
reflects this characteristic equation. Surely more important than
the isolated characterization of Cleopatra, in any case, is the
contrast provided by the food imagery between her and Caesar.
Neither is Antony excluded in the dramatic interaction of the
food images. The single effect Clemen sees in the images is
glimpsed in his lack of distinction between two of his examples
of Cleopatra's "lowest level": "I was/ A morsel for a monarch!"
(I, v, 30-31) and "I found you as a morsel, cold upon/ Dead
Caesar's trencher" (III, xiii, 116-117). Yet the echo calls for a
contrast more than a comparison. In the first of these lines Cleopatra is contrasting the physical prime of her salad days with
her maturity, when she is "with Phoebus' amorous pinches black,/
And wrinkled deep with time" (I, v, 28-29). Not only does the
image here have more than this single effect, but carries within it
the seemingly contradictory effects of emphasizing the physical
nature of her maturity by reminding us of her past, and yet contrasting her present with her purely physical past. She tells us in
the context of this first speech that "great Pompey" (l. 31) would
look at her "and die/ With looking on his life" (ll. 33-34). The
image here serves to contrast her purely physical relation to
Pompey and Julius Caesar with her fuller relationship with Antony, and yet to remind us that her relationship with Antony is
not wholly spiritual. Her affairs with Pompey and Caesar never
attained the fire and air of her love for Antony. The sexual pun
on die (l. 33), moreover, is echoed with pathetic power in her
plea to the literally dying Antony to die when he has lived ("Die
when thou hast liv'd", IV, xv, 38).[118]

The second of Clemen's examples, on the other hand, is part
of Antony's ranting to Cleopatra after she has offered her hand
to Thidias to kiss (III, xiii, 81 ff.). This example is not, as Clemen
would have it, one of Cleopatra on her "lowest level". Our sym-
pathies here are with her, not with Antony. While Thidias' request

[118]   Although Pope emends the line to read "where" in place of "when",
"when" is the only Folio reading. See IV, xv, 38n.

to kiss Cleopatra's hand probably takes its cue from her "I kiss his conquering hand" (l. 75), Cleopatra's comment (like her "Sole sir o' the world') [119] is an ironic one and part of her plan to "unpolicy" Caesar. But this scene with Thidias has been a misunderstood as her scene with Seleucus (V, ii, 140 ff.).[120] Realizing Cleopatra's attitude toward Octavius and the unreasonableness of Antony's railing (III, xiii, 34-152), we can hope that he will pause long enough for Cleopatra to explain. She tries (l. 109), but her attempt is in vain and we wonder, like Cleopatra, what their great love has come to (l. 115; cf. Antony in IV, xii, 20). We can only wait with her until his rage is gone (l. 153), but must still feel that by this point in the play Antony is foolish not to know her better (l. 157) than to think she would bow to Octavius, especially through "one that ties his points" (l. 157). Even Ovid, who admits his passion is "All-embracing" and that "There's not a sweetheart in town I'd be reluctant to love",[121] abhors "a servile slut" and asks,

> What man, born free, would ever twine
> His arms around a waist the lash has cut? [122]

Indeed, nothing makes Cleopatra's repeated distaste for Octavius more clear than the food imagery. Surely the bounty of the Alexandrine feasts (II, ii, 76; II, ii, 177; II, vii, 95; IV, ii, 10) contrasts with the "gross diet" of the Roman mob (V, ii, 210-211) and of Caesar (V, ii, 7-8). The contrast between the mere need or dependence upon food (cf. *Lear*, II, iv, 267 ff.) that is a beasts's as well as man's and the artistic enjoyment of food and music of the Egyptian Bacchanals (II, vii, 103) also serves to

---

[119]   See discussion, Chapter II.
[120]   Both Cleopatra's specifically and unnecessarily calling forth her treasurer (V, ii, 139) and her subsequent revelation to us that her plans are already provided (l. 194) argue for her fidelity to Antony. The importance of her calculated calling forth of Seleucus is emphasized since he is present only "by chance" in Plutarch (II, 130). Here too, however, we are told that Caesar supposed "he had deceived her, but indeed he was deceived himself" (II, 131). Cf. Brents Stirling, "Cleopatra's Scene with Seleucus: Plutarch, Daniel, and Shakespeare", *Shakespeare Quarterly*, XV (Spring, 1964), 299-311.
[121]   Ovid, "The Loves", IV, 47-48.
[122]   *Ibid.*, VII, 20-22.

contrast Cleopatra's world with Caesar's. The negative quality of Caesar's attitude toward food, moreover, is not to be confused with the heroic abstemiousness of Antony's past soldiership (I, iv, 55-71). Ironically at the end of the play, it is Cleopatra, who, refusing to be dependent upon food, says, "I'll eat no meat" (V, ii, 49), after Caesar admonishes her to "feed and sleep" (l. 186). Although Partridge points out both that "meat" originally meant "all food" and that it might also mean "the flesh of a wanton or a whore", he attributes no other sexual connotations or possible meanings to the word. Clearly, however, the line is part of the ascent to fire and air. Her line here, enforced by "Now no more/ The juice of Egypt's grape shall moist this lip" (ll. 280-281), is part of her new role as Antony's spiritual wife (l. 286). She will abstain from sexual relations (as well as from food) with all but the husband she hopes to join, and she means to share him with no one, including Iras (ll. 300 ff.).

Thus, while the food images in the play have been noted in creating atmosphere and in isolated characterizations, they have not been observed as demonstrating the interactions of either characterization or theme. It is much more significant in the play, for example, that Cleopatra is contrasted with both Caesar and all other women, for they cloy the "appetites" they feed. She alone makes "hungry,/ Where most she satisfies" (II, ii, 235-236).[123] The contrasts are more dramatically important than the single fact that Cleopatra is a salted morsel (II, i, 21). Most important, however, is that the food imagery is primarily sexual. The proverbial fact that Ceres and Bacchus precede Venus [124] (understood by everyone who has ever been intoxicated or hungry) is dramatized in Antony's line, "Love, I am full of lead:/ Some

---

[123]   Cf. *Venus and Adonis*, ll. 19-22:
    And yet not cloy thy lips with loath'd satiety,
    But rather famish them amid their plenty,
    Making them red and pale with fresh variety,
    Ten kisses short as one, one long as twenty.
  Cf. *Venus and Adonis*, l. 548 and Sonnets 56 and 118 for the same idea.
[124]   See entries under C211 in Morris Palmer Tilley, *A Dictionary of the Proverbs in England in the Sixteenth and Seventeenth Centuries* (Ann Arbor, University of Michigan Press, 1950), pp. 90-91. Cf. Burton, III, 218; Ovid, "The Art of Love", I, 229 ff.

wine within there, and our viands!" (III, xi, 72-73). Burton points out that idleness is a great incentive to love [125] (cf. I, ii, 127; I, iii, 90-95; I, v, 1-6); but "diet alone is able to cause it",[126] he says. Hunger, on the other hand, is offered as one of his cures for love.[127] Indeed, one of Burton's own images not only demonstrates the sexual possibilities of food imagery, but strikingly parallels some of the images of the play:

> The lascivious dotes on his fair mistress, the glutton on his dishes, which are infinitely varied to please the plate, the epicure on his several pleasures, the superstitious on his idol, and fats himself with future joys, as *Turks* feed themselves with an imaginary persuasion of a sensual Paradise; so several pleasant objects diversely affect divers men.[128]

The banquet imagery in *Antony and Cleopatra* is utilized primarily to demonstrate the sexual basis of a love ultimately stronger than the love of friendship or the love of a social and political marriage. The primary purpose is not merely to create tone or to show that Cleopatra was a good cook.

Even more obviously sexual in the play is the cluster of sword images, which have been pointed to almost exclusively as representative of Antony's past military glory. Yet the images often carry more phallic than military connotations. Thus, for example, one wonders at the critic's failure to notice the sexual connotations with Cleopatra's assertion at Antony's death,

> O, wither'd is the garland of the war,
> The soldier's pole is fall'n: young boys and girls
> Are level now with men . . . .
>
> (IV, xv, 64-66)

While "standard", "star" (cf. IV, xiv, 106), and "pole in a village festivity",[129] have all been suggested as readings for "soldier's

---

[125]   Burton, III, 70. (Cf. Burton, III, 69 and III, 119; Ovid, "The Remedies for Love", ll. 135-170; Castiglione, p. 242. Also see "love-in-idleness" (*A Midsummer-Night's Dream*), II, i, 168.)

[126]   *Ibid.*

[127]   *Ibid.*, III, 200.

[128]   *Ibid.*, III, 23.

[129]   See IV, xv, 65n in both the New Arden and Variorum editions of the play.

pole", no one has proposed the falling of the phallus as analogous to Antony's sexual and literal death. Traversi's comment is typical:

"The soldier's pole" is probably the Roman standard of war; but "pole" taken with "crown" and the following "boys and girls," bears a complex suggestion of May Day, when youthful love and the renewed life of spring meet annually in triumph. If we set these joyful associations against the corresponding depths of desolation, we shall feel something of the tremendous emotional range compassed by Cleopatra's utterance.[130]

Surely, however the "complex suggestions" of May include its phallic rites as well, and the "emotional range" of Cleopatra's utterance surely includes her awareness of the physical loss of Antony as well as the spiritual. The critics have remained as securely immune to any such reading of the lines, however, as the spinster teacher who fondly watches her girls around the maypole, unaware of its origins in fertility rites. Even Partridge's "comprehensive" glossary omits "pole", although the idea of young boys and girls now being level with men recalls "As well a woman with an eunuch play'd,/ As with a woman" (II, v, 5-6). The sexual basis of love is thus dramatized in bawdy puns as well as literally presented in the lines or enacted in scenes. The added and significant sexual reading again makes the lines richer. Here, for example, the sexual reading adds new meanings to the use of both "withered"[131] and "level". The sexual implications of Antony's "dying" are again dramatized in V, i, when Decertas enters *"with the sword of ANTONY"* (SD ff. 1. 3).

While Charney is perhaps the only critic to have studied the significantly sexual overtones of Antony's weapon, the sexual connotations of the very word "weapon" are clear in Shakespeare.[132] Even Charney, however, overlooks the extent to which the sexual parallels are drawn in the play, and Partridge mentions only one sexual use of the "sword" in the play. Often every

130 Traversi, *The Roman Plays*, p. 184.
131 Cf. "withered pear" from *All's Well* cited in Partridge.
132 Cf., for example, *II Henry IV*, II, i, 17 and II, iv, 120 ff. Also Cf. *Hamlet*, III, ii, 259-260: "It would cost you a groaning to take off my edge." See entries under "sword", "pistol", and "weapon" in Partridge.

reading but the obvious sexual one is offered. Thus, for example, when Antony warns Cleopatra "by my sword" (I, iii, 82), she responds to his "by my sword, –" with "And target". J. Dover Wilson with characteristic ingenuity and insight comments, thus "making it a swashbuckler's oath" comparable to *I Henry IV*, iii, 230.[133] But a more apt comparison is surely Juliet's speaking of herself as a "sheath" for Romeo's dagger at her "death" (V, iii, 169-170). Of course, Cleopatra literally is offering herself to be killed if Antony will dare do it. She can thus tell him both that she loves him enough not to want to live without him and also that she fears him not. But the Freudian symbolism of the sword (the "my" is merely Rowe's editorial conjecture) and target was surely apparent to the pre-Freudian members of Shakespeare's audience. If Charney, like Partridge, notes the sexual overtones of "She made great Caesar lay his sword to bed,/ He plough'd her and she cropp'd" (II, ii, 227-228), he ignores the equally sexual overtones of the echo in IV, xiv, 23, when Antony exclaims "She has robb'd me of my sword." The sexual (or loss of sexual) reading of the line is enforced when Mardian, the eunuch, enters immediately after the line is delivered.[134] We might even suggest that her forcing "great Caesar to lay his sword to bed", explains why he wears it "e'en like a dancer" (III, xi, 36) at Philippi. Now that he is old and withered and away from Cleopatra, he wears his sword, like a dancer, for decorative purposes only. He has no other purpose for it in life. Charney reads sexually Cleopatra's lines, "Then put my tires and mantles on him, whilst/ I wore his sword Philippan" (II, v, 22-23), but he misses the sexual point. Charney feels that these lines, strengthened by "Hush! Here comes Antony" (I, ii, 76; See I, ii, 76n), which is followed by Cleopatra's entrance, contribute to the picture of Antony's "effemination" [135] in the play. The effect of the line, however, is more one of Knight's "mingling or blending of the sexes" than of their confusion. It is more what Daiches calls a

[133]   See I, iii, 82n.
[134]   Cf. discussion in Chapter II of Antony's description as the bellows and the fan to cool a gypsy's lust followed by the entrance of Cleopatra fanned by eunuchs.
[135]   Charney, p. 130. See discussion, Chapter IV.

search for identity or sovereignty as opposed to the loss of identity
in union that is being dramatically discussed here.[136] Indeed, the
hint of effeminacy in Antony's boyhood suggested in Plutarch [137]
is deleted by Shakespeare. After all, Antony's wearing Cleopatra's tires and being compared to a eunuch are caused by his
masculine drives. He says himself to Cleopatra:

> You did know
> How much you were my conqueror, and that
> My sword, made weak by my affection, would
> Obey it on all cause.
>   (III, xi, 65-68)

The many bawdy puns in the play strengthen the dramatization
of the sexual nature of love seen in the phallic serpent and sword
images. Except for an occasional note on the word "dying", however, few sexual puns in the play have been commented upon.
Yet they include even those on eunuchs playing billiards (II, v,
3-6).[138] Even the obviously erotic implications of Antony's servant's name, "Eros", have gone virtually unnoticed.[139] Yet in
Antony's attempt at death in IV, xiv, Eros' name (although he
is not being introduced as a new character) is used six times by
Antony in the course of a single speech (ll. 35-54). The fact that
Eros is so called in Shakespeare's source [140] in no way alters the
emphasis selected by an artist obviously conscious of its overtones.[141] The many puns on "come", "welcome", and "dying",
hardly allow room for objections to overreading. Yet Partridge
gives no example from *Antony and Cleopatra* for the sexual puns
on either "coming" [142] or "dying". While we have often noted

[136] See discussion of sovereignty and union in love, Chapter IV.
[137] See Plutarch, II, 2. The Variorum selection of Plutarch (like Shakespeare) deletes this section.
[138] See II, v, 3n. Also see "billiards" in Partridge.
[139] Yet see "eros" in Partridge, who notes the punning name, but fails
to make any comment upon its functions.
[140] Plutarch, II, 121. The name is used twice here by Antony and once
in the exposition that precedes his use of the name. See the discussion of
Eros' name in the love-act structure, Chapter V.
[141] The significance of names has not often been noted in Shakespeare,
yet Malvolio, Jacques, Bottom, and Angelo all attest to "Will's" punning
use of names (even his own throughout his Sonnet sequence).
[142] See discussion, Chapter V.

that the critics have seen the pun in "I am dying, Egypt, dying", they have failed to note the many times it echoes in the play. Indeed, it recurs from the first to the last acts. When Enobarbus notes sardonically that "she hath such a celebrity in dying" (I, ii, 141-142),[143] it is clear (ll. 130-140) that he is aware of the sexual *doubles entendres*. While Caesar, on the other hand, may not be aware at the end of the play of the aptness of his punning, "She hath pursued conclusions infinite/ Of easy ways to die" (V, ii, 353-354), we as audience are. The repetitions of the pun in Antony's loving death and Cleopatra's death scene are too numerous to be disregarded.[144] The explicit clarifications of Plutarch that Cleopatra studies poisons for literal killing alone,[145] reveal Shakespeare's emphasis on the sexual nature of the puns. The pun may even underlie Cleopatra's "Can Fulvia die" (I, iii, 58), for this harsh accusation is one of which Cleopatra is fully capable at the moment. On a lower level, the line itself finds its parallel in Charmian's harsh and punning wish that Alexas "marry a woman that cannot go" (I, ii, 60-61).[146]

Too often both these comic and bawdy elements in the play have been avoided out of either prudishness or ignorance. Once the comedy and bawdry are sufficiently noticed, however, an analysis shows their functions to extend beyond the isolated tone or characterization to the themes of the play as a whole. The comedy and bawdry function in the interactions of tone, characterization, imagery, structure, and theme. The functions of the bawdry, like those of the comedy discussed above, are manifold. They include a dramatization of the sexual basis of love (the earth and water) upon which spiritual love (fire and air) is built. Neither are these sexual elements erased in the progress of the "ascending scale" toward spiritual love.[147] While Cleopatra as fire

---

[143] Cf. *Caesar*: "let the old ruffian know,/ I have many other ways to die" (IV, i, 4-5).

[144] See discussion, Chapter V.

[145] Plutarch, II, 114 ff.

[146] Partridge glosses this line sexually, but has doubts about its meaning. See his discussion.

[147] See Knight, pp. 205, 218, 219, 243.

and air may leave her other elements to baser life (V, ii, 288-289), there is still the trail of the Nile's "slime" on the fig-leaves (ll. 349-351) at the end of the play.

IV

THE NATURE OF LOVE AS A DRAMATIZED
THEME IN THE PLAY

> O, know, sweet love, I always write of you,
> And you and love are still my argument ...,
> (Sonnet 76)

wrote the "mellifluous & hony-tongued" author of the "sugred Sonnets".[1] Indeed, so penetrated with love are his early and popular *Venus and Adonis, The Rape of Lucrece*, and *Sonnets* that Meres proposed that "the sweete wittie soule of *Ouid*"[2] lived in the young poet. Yet the few studies of the theme of love in Shakespeare have been both superficial and condescending.[3] Periodically a book on "Shakespeare's attitude" toward love appears. In 1921, for example, C. H. Herford published an essay on "Shakespeare's Treatment of Love and Marriage" to arrive at this description of "the Shakespearean norm of love":

Love is a passion, kindling heart, brain, and sense alike in natural and happy proportions; ardent but not sensual,[4] tender but not sentimental, pure but not ascetic, moral but not puritanic, joyous but not frivolous, mirthful and witty but not cynical. His lovers look forward to marriage as a matter of course, and they neither anticipate its rights[5] nor turn their affections elsewhere.[6]

[1] Meres, p. 282.
[2] *Ibid.*
[3] But see Burton, III, 2: "I ought not to excuse or repent myself of this subject [love], on which many grave and worthy men have written whole volumes...." The impressive list continues through p. 7.
[4] One wonders, then, if Herford considers what Romeo and Juliet feel for each other as "love".
[5] Surely Juliet and Claudio in *Measure for Measure*, if not Angelo and Mariana by the end of the play (both pairs of whom anticipate the rights of marriage) are "in love."
[6] C. H. Herford "Shakespeare's Treatment of Love and Marriage" in

The *Times Literary Supplement* article provoked by Herford's book attests to "Shakespeare's place among the foremost of the poets of love".⁷ To support its view, the article cites the evidence of both tradition and the text:

Tradition, the popular voice, the judgment of the critics are at one in regarding Shakespeare as the poet of the earthly felicity of love. For this he was "sweet" and "gentle" in his own day, as he is in ours. The evidence of the plays is beyond all doubt. It is not a question of scattered lines or single characters, but of the general sentiment pervading all his plays; it cannot be escaped; it is the very air we breathe in them.⁸

But in the same article the comment is made (and it is one, unfortunately, with which many critics would agree) that "during the great tragedies love had been on the whole – save in *Antony and Cleopatra* – a subordinate issue".⁹ Yet even rejected love is more than "a subordinate issue" in *Hamlet*. And love is hardly subordinate in *Lear* or *Othello*. Shakespeare was never far from his argument of love, whether in *A Midsummer-Night's Dream, All's Well That Ends Well, Romeo and Juliet, The Tempest,* or *What You Will (Twelfth Night).*

Still, only two works since 1921 have conscientiously explored the love theme. In 1945 Herman Harrell Horne published a work on the ambitious, if not impossible, topic of *Shakespeare's Philosophy of Love*. In an effort to avoid the contradictions of the philosophy or philosophies dramatized in the different, unified works of art, Horne approaches each play in a separate, but short, chapter. The chapter on *Antony and Cleopatra,* for example, neatly categorizes "Shakespeare's attitude" in the play as "Wanton Love":

Shakespeare seems to be saying to us: Love has been like that, love may be like that, but love does not have to be like that. ... Shakespeare is not didactic; he is an artist who feels and depicts. In making

"Shakespeare's Treatment of Love and Marriage" and Other Essays (London, Adelphi Terrace, 1921), p. 18.
⁷ "Shakespeare and Love" in *The London Times Literary Supplement,* 13 October 1921 (Lead article, unsigned), p. 649.
⁸ *Ibid.*
⁹ *Ibid.,* p. 650.

us feel and see, he may also lead us, unintentionally on his part, into certain kinds of resolution and behavior.[10]

Curiously, however, both Horne and Herford, who speak of "Shakespeare's attitude" toward love and marriage, neglect mentioning Shakespeare's leaving his wife to go to London or the possible slight in his bequeathing her his "secondbest bed".[11]

In 1954 a third and equally generalized study was published by William G. Meader. His book, *Courtship in Shakespeare. Its Relation to the Tradition of Courtly Love,* belongs to those studies which treat Shakespeare's attitudes toward love as synonymous with the "predominant views" of his time. In his doctoral dissertation in 1955, Jack Suberman sees this predominant view as Platonic,[12] rather than that of Courtly Love, while an even more recent dissertation at Yale offers still another choice seeing *Antony and Cleopatra* as an anticipation of the tradition of Worldly Love.[13] But the common end of these studies seems to be a discovery of the source of Shakespeare's ideas of love, rather than an understanding of the ideas within the play. Shakespeare's knowledge and use of Plato is placed in its proper perspective by Edward Hubler:

---

[10]   Herman Harrell Horne, *Shakespeare's Philosophy of Love* (Raleigh, North Carolina, Edwards and Broughton Company, 1945), p. 152.

[11]   Sir Sidney Lee, "William Shakespeare" in *The Dictionary of National Biography,* ed. Sir Leslie Stephen and Sir Sidney Lee (Oxford, University Press, 1921-22), XVII, 1321.

[12]   Jack Suberman, *Platonism in Shakespeare* (Unpublished Ph.D. dissertation, University of North Carolina, 1955). While studies of Shakespeare's Platonism as reflected in his plays have been the subject of a number of studies, most have been cursory at best. See, for example, James D. Butler's "Shakespeare and Plato" in *Shakespeariana,* II (1885), 444-446 and his equally short "Platonic Allusions in Shakespeare" in *Shakespeariana,* III (1886), 230-232. See also John Vyvyan's *Shakespeare and Platonic Beauty* (London, Chatto and Windus, 1961); Frances A. Yates's "Shakespeare and the Platonic Tradition" in *University of Edinburgh Journal,* XII (1942-43), 2-12; Sears Reynolds Jayne's *Platonism in English Drama of the Renaissance* (1442-1642) (Unpublished Ph.D. dissertation, Yale University, 1948); and Walter Clyde Curry's *Shakespeare's Philosophical Patterns* (Baton Rouge, Louisiana, University Press, 1959).

[13]   Lenora Leet, *Elizabethan Love Tragedy. Patterns of Love Tragedy from Marlowe to Middleton: 1587-1622.* (Unpublished Ph.D. dissertation, Yale University, 1959.)

Nor is it necessary for Shakespeare to have studied the neo-Platonists of his time. He is not a philosopher, except in the sence in which philosophy is, as with Plato, the love of wisdom. He came by his ideas in the common and manifold ways of the literate, intelligent, gregarious man.[14]

Indeed, neo-Platonic ideas had already become so well known by Shakespeare's contemporaries that it would have been more difficult to avoid, than to be aware of them. Shakespeare could no more avoid such ideas as "the other half" or "love at first sight", for example, than could an illiterate, unintelligent, gregarious modern teenager who ever heard a jukebox play.

Even in those rare studies in which *Antony and Cleopatra* has been seen as a play about love, it has been viewed as a play limited to the love of "mature people". Coleridge, for example, suggests that the play be read in contrast to *Romeo and Juliet*, Shakespeare's play of Young Love, as opposed to this play about Love in Manhood.[15] Mark Van Doren reflects a widespread critical assumption when he says that "as lovers go, then, they are old".[16] Even more typical of the attitude of the critics is Oliver Emerson's observation that Antony and Cleopatra are "long past the pardonable warmth of youth".[17] E. E. Stoll excludes any judgment of them by writing only of *Shakespeare's Young Lovers*,[18] While Austin Wright sees the effect of the "autumnal love" [19] of Antony and Cleopatra as "salutary" for young people, who too often view thirty-two as the freezing point in the love of men.[20] Despite the critical emphasis upon the old age of the lovers which views their romance as a kind of January-January romance, only the harshest of Antony's critics in Rome reprove him for his "dotage" (I, i, 1; III, x, 20). The only other times the problem of age is introduced, it is broached by Antony and Cleopatra them-

[14]   Hubler, p. 71.
[15]   Coleridge, II, 319.
[16]   Van Doren, p. 239.
[17]   Oliver Farrar Emerson, "Antony and Cleopatra", *Poet Lore*, II (1890), 126.
[18]   Elmer Edgar Stoll, *Shakespeare's Young Lovers* (New York, Oxford University Press, 1937).
[19]   Austin Wright, p. 40.
[20]   *Ibid.*, p. 68.

selves. Enobarbus, a bitter critic at times, never uses the word. Although Cleopatra speaks of her "salad days" as past, she never seems concerned with age (which, after all, cannot wither her) except when she wonders at Octavia's. Indeed, she seems pleased that Octavia is thirty (III, ii, 28) [21] and speaks contemptuously of her own salad days, when, she realizes, she was "green in judgment, cold in blood" (I, v, 74). Antony himself worries that he may "lose myself in dotage" (I, ii, 114), but the emphasis is upon the strength of the fetters that bind him (l. 113), not on his age.[22] The only other time that Antony mentions his "doting", he speaks not only of his white hairs, but of his brown ones as well (III, xi, 13-15). He emphasizes this mixture of his grey and brown hairs to Cleopatra later in the play:

> What, girl, though grey
> Do something mingle with our younger brown, yet ha' we
> A brain that nourishes our nerves, and can
> Get goal for goal of youth.
>
> (IV, viii, 19-22)

The fact also remains that if Antony is not of Romeo's age, neither is Cleopatra of Juliet's. This is no January-May comic romance. Shakespeare's source gives us this information concerning their ages: "Cleopatra died being eight-and-thirty year old, after she had reigned two-and-twenty years, and governed above fourteen of them with Antonius. And for Antonius, some say that he lived three-and-fifty years: and others say, six-and-

[21]   Although Ridley comments that Cleopatra "passes on without comment" (III, iii, 28n), Cleopatra seems no less concerned by Octavia's being thirty than that Octavia's hair is brown (l. 32). For both these answers, she offers gold as a reward (l. 33). While Cleopatra does ask for both her rival's years and color of hair (II, v, 112-113), she does so in anticipation, it seems, of a very young girl, not of a widow about thirty. Ridley suggests that she makes no comment because she herself is thirty-eight, but Plutarch, not Shakespeare, says she is thirty-eight when she dies and after she has reigned twenty-two years (see discussion below) with Antony. If her own hair is not entirely brown, it is only, like Antony's "something" mingled with gray (IV, viii, 19-20). Plutarch speaks further of "Cleopatra, who neither excelled Octavia in beauty, nor yet in young years" (II, 91).
[22]   The word "doting", moreover, often suggests the foolish intensity of loving too well, rather than age. See, for example, the word as it applies to the hardly aged Beatrice and Benedick (*Much Ado*, II, iii, 99 and 219).

fifty." [23] According to Plutarch, then, Cleopatra was twenty-four when she met Antony, who was then either thirty-nine or forty-two. Plutarch further notes that when Antony met Cleopatra, she was "at age when a woman's beauty is at the prime, and she also of best judgment." [24] Shakespeare's play hardly mentions Cleopatra's age (at least not as often as Plutarch's account). His Cleopatra can even jokingly view herself as "wrinkled deep in time" (I, v, 29), for she is self-assured by her attractiveness to Antony (l. 25) now as well as by her youthful conquests of Caesar (ll. 29-31) and "great Pompey" (l. 31).

Too often, moreover, when the difference in age between Romeo and Antony is noted by the critics, that difference is seen to reflect Shakespeare's own aging. M. R. Ridley, for example, speaks of *Antony and Cleopatra* as "in a sense the *Romeo and Juliet* of a mature man". That the "mature man" here spoken of is Shakespeare and not Antony is clear in Ridley's observation that completes his sentence: "that the man who wrote the one play could within twelve or thirteen years write the other shows the bitter rapidity of the maturing".[25] In addition to Shakespeare's being closer to Antony's age than to Romeo's when he wrote *Romeo and Juliet*, we should also note that autumnal lovers were not necessarily looked on harshly by even the young writer of the Sonnets. Sonnet 45 ("That time of year thou mayst in me behold"), for example, probably written about the time of *Romeo and Juliet*, hardly elicits an unsympathetic reaction toward its *persona*. Shakespeare's characters, like Peter Bembo in Castiglione's *The Courtier*, present at least the possibility [26] that mature men and women can be in love.[27] Ovid speaks of the advantages of old lovers,[28] and Burton enumerates their superior knowledge of love by citing Stefano Guazzo, who says that

an old, a grave, discreet man, is fittest to discourse of Love matters, because he hath likely more experience, observed more, hath a more

[23] Plutarch, II, 135.
[24] *Ibid.*, II, 38.
[25] Ridley, pp. vii-viii.
[26] See discussion of question structure, Chapter V.
[27] Castiglione, pp. 303 and 312.
[28] Ovid, "The Art of Love", II, 693-702.

staid judgement, can better discern, resolve, discuss, advise, give better cautions, and more solid precepts, better inform his auditors in such a subject, and by reason of his riper years sooner divert.[29]

When Burton speaks harshly of old men or old women as lovers, it is only when they choose ridiculously younger objects for their love.[30] Even Socrates, after all, was taught love by the old Diotima.[31]

If some have viewed the play as one concerned wholly with old lovers, others have seen love as a subordinate, if not incidental, theme in the play. Some, for example, have seen the love theme as the necessary, but baser, alternative to duty. Love is seen only as it distracts or tempts Antony from the "nobler" aspects of life. Arthur Symons, for example, describes the play as "the eternal tragedy of love and ambition, and here, for once, it is the love which holds by the baser nature of the man who is the subject of it, the ambition which is really the prompting of his nobler side".[32] Symons' view of the play is essentially that of Dryden's *All for Love, or the World Well Lost*. In his comment that "this is a play about politics, and very ugly politics, as much as it is a play about love",[33] Austin Wright at least grants love an equal share of the play with "ugly politics". Bethell also speaks of love and politics as providing the essential conflict of the play:

While the two themes of love and empire are thus paralleled in power and grandeur, they are at the same time sharply contrasted as conflicting alternatives presented to Antony's choice. The contrast is geographically expressed, as between East and West, or Egypt and Rome, "Cleopatra" and "Egypt" are almost synonymous. ... Octavius Caesar stands for the Roman qualities as Cleopatra does for the Egyptian.[34]

But such a description reflects Plutarch's account of "The Life of Marcus Antonius" more than it does Shakespeare's play about

---

[29] Burton, III, 2.
[30] *Ibid.*, III, 61-62.
[31] Plato, pp. 66 ff.
[32] Symons, p. 5.
[33] Austin Wright, p. 38.
[34] Bethell, p. 120.

the love of Antony and Cleopatra. The play is not Antony's story, with Cleopatra but one of Antony's choices.[35]

If some would see love as but one choice of Antony, however, others would deny the very name of love to the passion of Antony and Cleopatra. Stempel, Dowden, and Bryant agree that it is lust.[36] Croce and Boas agree only that it is not love; Croce terms it "voluptuousness"[37] and Boas labels it "sexual passion".[38] Lloyd calls it "folly to attempt to force upon Antony's pleasure (II, iii, 39-40) the interpretation of love".[39] Emerson categorizes the relationship as "a sensual amour, but with no trust, no real sympathy, no depth of affection. Their ruin and death are due to their own guilty passion, and to causes wholly within themselves".[40] "Antony and Cleopatra'", he continues

shows only love's debased coin; the kiss of Antony is that of a profligate, bestowed on one who receives it only with soiled lips and an empty heart. Antony gives himself to Cleopatra's charms; Cleopatra captivates Antony for her own sensual pleasure, and, less distinctly, for her own love of power.[41]

While the death scenes of the protagonists obviously argue for more "trust", "sympathy", and selflessness than the "soiled lips" in the style of a cheap novel, the question of lust is surely one of the questions of the play.[42] The question of the relationship between love and lust or of their mutual exclusiveness is one common to Renaissance discussions of love.[43]

[35] See discussion, Chapter II.

[36] Stempel, p. 66; Dowden, p. 278; and Bryant, p. 174.

[37] Benedetto Croce, *Ariosto, Shakespeare, and Corneille*, trans. Douglas Ainslie (New York, Henry Holt and Company, 1920), p. 244.

[38] Frederick S. Boas, *Shakspere and his Predecessors* (New York, Charles Scribner's Sons, [n.d.]), p. 477.

[39] Lloyd, p. 88.

[40] Emerson, p. 126.

[41] *Ibid.*

[42] Cf. Stirling, p. 159: "It is interesting that Shakespeare seems to have anticipated the problem of sexual infatuation as a tragic theme by actually posing the question as a theme within the play." See discussion of question structure, Chapter V.

[43] See, for example, the dialogue between Sophia and Philo on love and desire which forms the entire First Dialogue (pp. 1-64) of Leone Ebreo's *Dialoghi d'Amore*. Sophia contends that love and desire are mutually ex-

These critics who have termed the relationship of Antony and Cleopatra one of love have condemned by faint praise. Ridley, for example, soon echoes the very objections of Emerson in his "justification" of the use of the word "love":

It is the merest fatuity of moralizing to deny the name of "love" to their passion, and write it off as "mere lust." No doubt it is not the highest kind of love; it is completely an *egoisme a deux*, and has no power to inspire to anything outside itself; but it has in it something that should be an element in the highest kind of love; and at least it is the passion of human beings and not of animals, of the spirit as well as of the body.[44]

Ridley's implied condemnation of bodily love reflects his view, which holds ideas of love valid when they coincide with his own, a common approach to ideas of love in the play.[45] The "at least", for example, that Ridley feels compelled to add seems to show his personal preference for a love composed entirely of the spirit (and totally devoid of the body). But *Antony and Cleopatra*, we have seen,[46] dramatizes the idea that a love solely spiritual (like Antony's and Octavia's) is not as "real" as the love (of Antony and Cleopatra) that grows to fire and air, but has its roots strongly based in earth and water.

Coleridge also grants the term "love" to the relationship of Antony and Cleopatra when he speaks of their play as part of "Shakespeare's double portrait of Love".[47] It contrasts specifically with *Romeo and Juliet*, he says, "as the love of passion and appetite opposed to the love of affection and instinct".[48] Behrens speaks of "Shakespeare's purpose" in *Antony and Cleopatra* as one to dramatize "the effect of unbridled, passionate, unreasoning love on two natures".[49] But if Othello tells us he was "lov'd

---

clusive while Philo asserts that they at least partially overlap. The discussion continues pp. 244 ff. See also Burton, III, 10, 14, 34, 84, 86, 235.
[44] Ridley, p. liii.
[45] See discussion, Chapter I.
[46] See discussion, Chapter III.
[47] Coleridge, II, 31.
[48] *Ibid.*, I, 86.
[49] Ralph Behrens, "Cleopatra Exonerated", *The Shakespeare Newsletter*, IX (November, 1959), 37.

not wisely but too well" (V, ii, 344), *Antony and Cleopatra* raises the double question of whether Reason and Love can exist simultaneously and whether it is possible to love at all if not too well.[50] MacCallum speaks of the love of Antony and Cleopatra with the same limitations as does Behrens: "Despite the sympathy with which Shakespeare regards Antony's passion both as an object of pursuit and as indication of nobility, he is quite aware that it is pernicious and criminal. Relatively it may be extolled: absolutely it must be condemned." [51] But like most other views of the play, MacCallum's relativity is not one that reflects the context of the play, while his Absolute is one that mirrors his own preconceived, moralizing views of love.

Indeed, those few critics who have seen any content in the dazzling *tour de force* [52] have subordinated or ignored the love theme. Bryant sees the play as an attempt through poetic creation to capture a dream of human dignity.[53] To Ivor Brown, *Antony and Cleopatra* is "essentially a play of forgiveness".[54] G. B. Harrison regards the play simply as a "sequel to *Julius Caesar*".[55] Perhaps the most common current view of the play (although any view of it as other than the fall of Antony is probably a recent one) is that of the conflict between the values of East and West. To Danby, for example, the conflict is seen as symbolic of the opposing natures of the Flesh (Cleopatra) and the World (Rome).[56] Bethell sees this conflict between East and West in a different light:

More generally – and more philosophically – we have in the contrast between Egypt and Rome, the old opposition with which Shakespeare was concerned in the comedies and in *Troilus and Cressida*, between "intuition" and "reason"; on the one hand the final authority of the

---

50   See discussion below.
51   MacCallum, p. 441.
52   See discussion, Chapter I.
53   Bryant, p. 174.
54   Brown, p. 185.
55   G. B. Harrison, "Introduction to *The Tragedy of Antony and Cleopatra*" in *Shakespeare's Complete Works* (New York, Harcourt, Brace and World, 1952), p. 1219.
56   Danby, p. 140.

spontaneous affections, on the other the authority of world wisdom or practical common sense . . . .[57]

The only study devoted exclusively to the love theme in *Antony and Cleopatra* is a short and generalized article of John Wilcox entitled "Love in *Antony and Cleopatra*". Rather than stressing the historical sources of Shakespeare's ideas of love, or the ideas as presented in the play itself, Wilcox's emphasis is on the psychological validity of Shakespeare's "personal" views of love. "Shakespeare's experience", he tells us, "like the observations of the modern psychologists [No specific psychologists are named, but "they" seem to agree with one another], affirmed the existence of opposing urges, the one toward love and the other toward a manly career." [58] Perhaps the most provocative idea, which Wilcox sees only as Shakespeare's precocious "modern psychological insight", is the problem of love attained. Once Cleopatra is attained, Wilcox says, Antony's thoughts turn away from his bliss to his neglected affairs.[59] "In his earlier plays", continues Wilcox, Shakespeare "has often reflected the immature view that the only problem in love is that of attaining." [60] But Wilcox might better reflect Shakespeare's famous impartiality by showing an awareness of the individuality of these earlier and separate works of art. We might also wonder whether or not "maturity" or psychological "normality" have characterized (or are even the goals of) the artist or his supposed views. But the problem of attainment in love is hardly a modern psychological discovery. Plato, Capellanus, Burton, and *Antony and Cleopatra* itself discuss the idea.[61]

If Wilcox's study is the only study of the play devoted exclusively to the love theme, Lord David Cecil gives us the reason why. Love, he asserts, is only a minor part of the play:

Finally, if love is meant to be the main theme, Shakespeare is shockingly careless about sticking to it. A large part of the plot has nothing to do with the lovestory. . . . No – if *Antony and Cleopatra*

[57] Bethell, p. 122.
[58] John Wilcox, "Love in *Antony and Cleopatra*", *Papers of the Michigan Academy of Science, Arts, and Letters*, XXI (1935), 535.
[59] *Ibid.*, p. 533.
[60] *Ibid.*, p. 543.
[61] See discussion below.

is meant to be a typical Shakespearean tragic drama, with love as its theme, it is a failure.[62]

Lord David contends that, while other dramatists and historians "concentrated exclusively on the love-story", this same love-story is seen in *Antony and Cleopatra* "always in its relation to the rivalry between Octavius and Antony".[63] Even a cursory reading of North's Plutarch, however, reveals Shakespeare's shift of emphasis toward the love-story and away from politics. As we have already noted and demonstrated,[64] moreover, the politics of the play are repeatedly viewed in the context of love (whether Antony's, Cleopatra's, Octavia's, or Pompey's). Indeed, the very language of love is utilized in the political world. While we have suggested some examples of this use of the language of love in the world of politics, the discussion might profitably be amplified here. The very word "love" and its many variations are used by and about most of the leaders of the Roman World. The Messenger, for example, relates to Caesar that "Pompey is strong at sea,/ And it appears he is belov'd of those/ That only have fear'd Caesar . . ." (I, iv. 36-38). The word "belov'd" recalls the distinction between the lover and beloved discussed in many treatises on love.[65] It is dramatically discussed elsewhere in the play when the Soothsayer predicts that Charmian will be "more beloving than belov'd" (I, ii, 22) as well as when Antony and Cleopatra are dubbed a "mutual pair" (I, i, 37).[66] Caesar's response to the messenger who gives the news of Pompey underscores the implications of Pompey in the love theme:

> I should have known no less;
> It hath been taught us from the primal state
> That he which is was wish'd, until he were;

[62] Lord David Cecil, p. 9.
[63] *Ibid.*, p. 13.
[64] See discussion, Chapter III.
[65] Leone Ebreo discusses the lover and the beloved, pp. 268 ff. Ovid in "The Art of Love" (I, 38-40) and Leone Ebreo (p. 149) both discuss the desirability of mutual love.
[66] Cf. Marsilio Ficino on simple and mutual love in "Commentary on Plato's *Symposium*" trans. Sears Reynolds Jayne, *University of Missouri Studies*, XIX (1944), 143.

> And the ebb'd man, ne'er lov'd till ne'er worth love,
> Comes dear'd, by being lack'd.
>
> (I, iv, 40-44)

The ideas of attainment and possession in love, the worth of the beloved, and the absence of the lover again introduce comparisons and contrasts with the mutual love of Antony and Cleopatra. Indeed, Antony has introduced this same idea of love for Pompey that Caesar echoes here:

> Our slippery people,
> Whose love is never link'd to the deserver
> Till his deserts are past, begin to throw
> Pompey the Great,[67] and all his dignities
> Upon his son . . . .
>
> (I, ii, 183-187)

Pompey himself, while primarily concerned with "the political" world of the play, often speaks of love. He is aware, for example, that "the people love me" (II, i, 9) and contrast himself with Lepidus, who "flatters both,/ Of both is flatter'd; but he neither loves,/ Nor either cares for him" (II, i, 14-16). Lepidus often serves in the play as a kind of political parallel to Octavia, who "neither way inclines" (III, ii, 50). At one point he is even described as a kind of love-sick damsel:

> Octavia weeps
> To part from Rome; Caesar is sad, and Lepidus,
> Since Pompey's feast, as Menas says, is troubled
> With the green-sickness.
>
> (III, ii, 3-6)

The green-sickness of love-sick maidens is one described at length by Burton.[68]

The parallels between love in politics and the love of love are manifold. When Menas offers Pompey all the world (II, vii, 61 ff.), for example, the offer is strikingly like Antony's declarations to Cleopatra (I, i; 15, 17, 39). Pompey's rejection of Menas' offer also forms a parallel to Cleopatra's rejection of Antony's

---

[67] See I, ii, 186n. The confusion between Sextus Pompey and Pompey the Great is noted here.
[68] Burton III, 154.

hyperbolic proposal (ll. 16 and 40 ff.). Had Menas merely delivered the proof of his love "and not have spoke on't" (l. 74),
Pompey tells us he would have it, as gladly, we should suppose,
as Cleopatra accepts all from Antony. The contrast between the
mere words of the purely idealized love of Octavia and the love
that grows into fire and air, but is grounded in the earth is also
reflected in the line. The progression in the play from the words
of the love-game to the real acts of love as the actions of the
lovers "move into harmony with their utterances"[69] is an important movement in the play. The words themselves, moreover,
are an important part of the progression to the epitome of love.[70]
The contrast between the loving words of Antony and Cleopatra
and Octavia, whose "tongue will not obey her heart, nor . . ./ Her
heart inform her tongue" (III, ii, 47-48) is hardly accidental.
Octavia's own brother underlines the role of ostentation in love
in a speech strikingly parallel to the ostentation of Cleopatra's
barge speech:

> Why have you stol'n upon us thus? You come not
> Like Caesar's sister: the wife of Antony
> Should have an army for an usher, and
> The neighs of horse to tell of her approach,
> Long ere she did appear. The trees by the way
> Should have borne men, and expectation fainted,
> Longing for what it had not. Nay, the dust
> Should have ascended to the roof of heaven,
> Rais'd by your populous troops: but you are come
> A market-maid to Rome, and have prevented
> The ostentation of our love; which, left unshown,
> Is often left unlov'd: we should have met you
> By sea, and land, supplying every stage
> With an augmented greeting.
>   (III, vi, 42-55)

But Octavia cannot speak of love. She can only say "Good night,
sir" (II, iii, 8) to Antony, or "I'll tell you in your ear" (III, ii, 46)
to her beloved brother. The effectiveness (even necessity) of
speaking of love and playing the love-game is an idea dramatized
by Rosalind and Orlando, if not by Beatrice and Benedick.

[69]   Murray, p. 378. Cf. Schwartz, p. 551 and discussion, Chapter III.
[70]   Cf. Castiglione, p. 237.

Even when Menas and the cynical Enobarbus speak to each other, the language is more of lovers than of warriors. After admitting, "I never lov'd you much" (II, vi, 76), Enobarbus characterizes the two of them as "two thieves kissing" (l. 96). When Menas answers that "All men's faces are true whatsome'er their hands are", Enobarbus responds more like the *persona* of Donne's *Songs and Sonets* than a cynical Roman soldier: "But there is never a fair woman has a true face." Despite the obvious relevance of beauty and fidelity to any serious discussion or dramatization of love, many like Lord David would deny such scenes as relevant to the love theme. The emphasis of the lines here is as much on love as those of Shakespeare's own Sonnet 105:

> "Fair, kind, and true" is all my argument,
> "Fair, kind, and true" varying to other words;
> And in this change is my invention spent,
> Three themes in one, which wondrous scope affords.
>   "Fair, kind and true" have often liv'd alone,
>   Which three till now never kept seat in one.

Enobarbus represents another kind of love in the play, the love of a friend as well as that of a loyal servant. Despite The Elizabethan Attitude that friendship is higher than love between man and woman, this is not the view dramatized in *Antony and Cleopatra*. Enobarbus, unlike Cleopatra, is not the equal of Antony. Antony can reprimand him for his light answers (I, ii, 174), and command him to speak no more, for he is, after all, "a soldier only" (II, ii, 107). Cleopatra alone is Antony's equal, and Hymen himself tells us

> Then is there mirth in heaven
> When earthly things made even
>   Atone together.
>
>   (*As You Like It*, V, iv, 114-116)

Cleopatra's love for Antony is greater than Enobarbus', moreover, not only because it includes comradeship within it,[71] but because it is proved by her constancy. Enobarbus' love, like Octavia's, alters when it alteration finds. Such love is not love (Son-

---

[71]   See discussion below.

net 116).[72] Enobarbus' love for Antony like Octavia's though inferior to Antony's and Cleopatra's, dramatizes another aspect of the nature of love.

The wars and politics of the play, despite Lord David's contentions, form the background of the play. This is most easily seen by what Shakespeare has omitted from Plutarch. At specific points in the play, however, the war serves to demonstrate the similarities between war and love that are commonplace, if not archetypal, in poetry. Ovid mentions the analogy in his discussions of love, for example.[73] Antony speaks lovingly to Cleopatra in images of war throughout the play, calling himself her soldier (I, iii, 70) and her "The armourer of my heart" (IV, iv, 7).[74] Even Caesar speaks in terms of *amour*. He dubs Antony "my mate in empire" (V, i, 43). He may even continue some of the sexual imagery (though unknowingly as character) when he speaks of Octavia as providing the "hoop" (II, ii, 115) to hold together "our loves" (l. 153) – if the hoop has any of the connotations that rings often have in Shakespeare's plays.[75] Pompey speaks of Caesar and Antony alike as "cuckolds" in having stolen the sovereignty by land from his father (II, vi, 26 ff.). Even the word "breed" in the political world (I, ii, 190; I, iii, 48) reinforces the dramatic purposes of the fertility images discussed in Chapter III.

While the play stresses the sexual basis of the love of Antony and Cleopatra, it does not portray it as exclusively physical. Some critics, however, have held this view of their relationship.[76] The comradeship of Antony and Cleopatra has been discussed only by S. E. Peart in a brief article in *Poet Lore* in 1892. Here Peart sums up what he feels is this most arresting quality of Cleopatra's infinite variety.

Was it her superior ability as a ruler of Egypt; or the fluency with which she conversed alike with Hebrews, Troglodites, Arabs, Syrians,

---

[72] See discussion below of what is not love.

[73] Ovid, "The Loves", IX, 1-46 and "The Art of Love", II, 230-250.

[74] Cf. Antony calling Cleopatra "my warrior" (IV, viii, 24), and Othello calling the mild Desdemona "my fair warrior" (II, i, 184).

[75] Cf. Partridge on the sexual connotations of "ring" in Shakespeare.

[76] See discussion of love and lust below and those who would deny the term "love" to their relationship above.

Medes, and Parthians? Was it her subtile wit, her fascinating manner? Was she more beautiful than all other women? No; not one nor all of these could so have enslaved a Caesar or an Antony as did this "serpent of old Nile." It was a trait, a faculty (call it what we may), most infrequently practised by woman, and then only by those of distinct individuality, – of being a real companion to man.[77]

MacCallum also notices, if only in passing, that "the devotion of Antony" is not merely "the devotion of a sonneteer; it is far more absolute and unquestioning, it is far more comrade-like and sympathetic".[78] But MacCallum, like Peart, bases his impression on Plutarch, feeling that "the original of Cleopatra is the Cleopatra of Plutarch".[79] While MacCallum offers no specific passages in Plutarch as evidence for his impression, the lines are there. Plutarch's Cleopatra plays at dice, drinks, and hunts with Antony.[80] Indeed, she even mocks his plain jests.[81] But the idea of comradeship is dramatized in Shakespeare's play as well. When Antony asks, "What sport to-night?" (I, i, 47), the meaning may be sexual, but the tone is that of a jovial companion to his equal. Cleopatra tells of the many "times" they had when

> I laugh'd him out of patience; and that night
> I laugh'd him into patience, and next morn,
> Ere the ninth hour, I drunk him to his bed;
> Then put my tires and mantles on him, whilst
> I wore his sword Philippan.
>
> (II, v, 19-23)

Antony and Cleopatra not only make love, they wander through the streets together (I, i, 52-53), they eat together, drink together, fish together, laugh together, and even fight (no matter how unsuccessfully) together.

Indeed, the comradeship of Antony and Cleopatra prevents their relationship from cloying. A purely sexual relationship would soon bore both of the hardly virginal protagonists.[82] An-

---

[77] S. E. Peart, "The Comradeship of Antony and Cleopatra", *Poet Lore*, IV (15 April 1892), 219.
[78] MacCallum, p. 314.
[79] *Ibid.*, p. 313.
[80] Plutarch, II, 43.
[81] *Ibid.*, II, 40.
[82] See discussion of love and lust below.

tony and Cleopatra repeatedly presents the Art of Love. While Caesar is portrayed as only reasonable, Charmian by losing all reason would, like a fool, teach the way for Cleopatra to lose Antony (I, iii, 10). Cleopatra, like Hamlet, is "but mad north-north-west" (II, ii, 396). Her "love is wise in folly, foolish-witty" (*Venus and Adonis*, l. 838). Love, then, the play would assert, in order not to cloy once the object has been obtained must be fashioned by the conscious craftmanship of art. The idea is both dramatized in Cleopatra's actions and debated in her discussions with Charmian. The idea is one discussed in most of the Medieval and Renaissance dialogues on love. Cleopatra's "crossing" (I, iii, 9) Antony at every turn both in word (e.g., ll. 64-65) and action (e.g., I, ii, 84) is but a dramatization of the idea of the Law of Love that "The easy attainment of love makes it of little value; difficulty of attainment makes it prized." [83] Once Antony possesses Cleopatra, her art must be employed in holding him, for

> Seeking is all very well, but holding requires greater
>   talent:
>   Seeking involves some luck; now the demand is for
>   skill.[84]

Indeed, many of the ideas in Shakespeare's teacher, Ovid, are those practiced by Cleopatra. She, for example, unlike Charmian, seems to have read his advice to "Let the occasional No! be an incentive to vows",[85] to tell lies and to weep at will,[86] and to "make a fool of her lovers".[87] Burton also discusses the necessity of Art to maintain love.[88] So while Ovid holds that a lover should "Laugh when she laughs", and "if she weeps, ... join her in weeping",[89] and Burton assigns the same advice to Plutarch,[90] Cleopatra's art is based rather on the attraction of opposites:

[83]   Andreas Capellanus, *The Art of Courtly Love*, trans. John Jay Parry (New York, Frederick Ungar, 1961), p. 27.
[84]   Ovid, "The Art of Love", II, 13-14.
[85]   *Ibid.*, XIX, 6.
[86]   *Ibid.*, XIX, 33.
[87]   Burton, III, 99 ff.
[88]   Ovid, "The Art of Love", II, 201.
[89]   Ovid, "The Loves", I, 85-86.
[90]   Plutarch in Burton, III, 59.

> If you find him sad,
> Say I am dancing; if in mirth report
> That I am sudden sick.
>
> (I, iii, 3-5)

Charmian, like Plutarch and Ovid, would "cross him in nothing" (l. 9). Nor is this idea of opposites in the Art of Love a new idea of the "mature Shakespeare":

> Being proud, as females are, to see him woo her,
> She puts on outward strangeness, seems unkind,
>   Spurns at his love and scorns the heat he feels,
>   Beating his kind embracements with her heels.
>
> (*Venus and Adonis*, ll. 309-312)

Thus, while some critics have contended that *Antony and Cleopatra* is about love only incidentally, we have seen a number of ideas on the structure of love dramatized in the play. We have already noticed the thematic implications of some of the bawdy puns and sexual images. We have seen enacted the idea that equals but opposites are attracted; and that love may progress from words to deeds, from a game to reality, and from sexual earth to spiritual fire. That "Love's reason's without reason" (*Cymbeline*, IV, ii, 22) and that reason is not all are still other themes we have seen presented in the play.[91] Both the sublime and foolish aspects of love are dramatized in *Antony and Cleopatra*,[92] as well as the roles of the beloved and the lover in a mutual relationship. Yet Lord David says that the play is not concerned with love.

Perhaps the most misunderstood of the lines concerning the nature of love are those of Cleopatra:

> I drunk him to his bed;
> Then put my tires and mantles on him, whilst
> I wore his sword Philippan.
>
> (II, v, 21-23)

While we have noted incidentally the comradeship in the drinking

---

[91]   See discussion of love and reason, Chapter III. Cf. Castiglione, p. 312 and Capellanus, p. 48.
[92]   See discussion, Chapter III.

and the foolish love play of the lines (and briefly discussed the
sword image in Chapter III), Stempel explicates the lines in terms
of The Elizabethan Attitude toward love. He points to the wearing
of men's attire by courtesans as a sign of degeneracy of the times
as remarked in Marston's *Second Satire*.[93] Rosen also observes
that "Cleopatra's exchange of garments with Antony and her
appropriation of his sword, symbol of manliness and soldierly
virtue, signify more than playful hilarity; they point to her dominance over him, and this is made explicit on many occasions." [94]
Stempel goes still farther to term Cleopatra's domination of Antony "an unnatural reversal of the roles of man and woman".[95]
"On the psychological level", he continues, "this change of values
corresponds to the similarly unnatural dominance of reason by
will in Antony's character, and, on the political level, it is mir-
rored by the struggle of Antony and Cleopatra against the rational
Octavius." [96] But in addition to both the playful hilarity and
Cleopatra's dominance of Antony, the lines also suggest Knight's
"blending of the sexes". The point is not so much Antony's
effeminacy or degeneration, as his union with Cleopatra. The
tone of this passage is not unlike Caesar's statement that Antony
"is not more manlike/ Than Cleopatra; nor the queen of Ptolemy/
More womanly than he . . ." (I, iv, 5-7). This blending of male
and female in a love union and the notion that lovers become like
the loved ones are topics in both Ficino's commentary on Plato's
Symposium and Leone Ebreo's *Diarloghi d'Amore*.[97] The active
or lover's role that is generally considered male is taken by
Cleopatra from the very beginning of their relationship when she
refuses Antony's invitation to dinner, inviting him instead to become her guest (II, ii, 219 ff.). Cleopatra retains this active role
when she sends to find out what mood Antony is in, but her
orders are that Antony is not to know of her lack of passivity.
"I did not send you" (I, iii, 3), she explains to Charmian. The
idea that a woman should behave in an active but secret manner

93 Stempel, p. 64.
94 Rosen, p. 144.
95 Stempel, p. 62.
96 *Ibid.*
97 Leone Ebreo, pp. 346 and 355 and Ficino, p. 227.

in order to gain a man is still echoed in the proverbial "A man
chases a woman until she catches him." Indeed, were Cleopatra
passive when Antony comes to leave her, she would surely have
lost him (I, iii, 13-105). Ovid in "The Loves" asks rhetorically,
"Isn't the best defense always a good attack?" [98] When Antony
approaches her, even after she is in the very act of sending for
him (I, ii, 82), she refuses to receive him as feminine passivity
demands: "We will not look upon him" (l. 84). Feminine though
she be, Cleopatra yearns to assume the masculine role, rather than
merely wait to be beloved. "I would I had thy inches" (I, iii, 40),
she exclaims, and the meanings of the line are manifold.[99] As a
Queen, Cleopatra is not to be considered an inferior like one of
Plato's women in the *Symposium*. She knows that she, "as the
president of my kingdom will/ Appear there for a man" (III, vii,
17-18). In much the same way that Cleopatra's aggressiveness
demonstrates her desire to be active rather than any lesbian ten-
dencies, Antony's domination by Cleopatra emphasizes not his
effeminacy but the paradox of love that that which most easily
demonstrates a man's masculinity, may also emasculate him. The
emasculation by excessive masculine pursuits we have seen dramatized in Antony's relation to Mardian.[100] In addition to the
equations with Mardian that we have already noted, Enobarbus
tells Cleopatra that Antony is

> Traduc'd for levity, and 'tis said in Rome
> That Photinus, an eunuch, and your maids
> Manage this war.
>
> (III, vii, 13-15)

Canidius then echoes this idea when he says "our leader's led,/
And we are women's men" (ll. 69-70). But Antony's soldiers are
no more effeminate, nor degenerate, than their leader. Occasionally such images do no more than demonstrate that tears are for
women, not soldiers. Thus, much like Macduff's apology for
coming to the brink of tears after his wife and children are killed
by Macbeth ("O, I could play the woman with mine eyes", IV,

[98]   Ovid, "The Loves", I, 80.
[99]   See discussion, Chapter II.
[100] See discussion, Chapter II.

iii, 230), Enobarbus exclaims, "And I, an ass, am onion-ey'd; for shame,/ Transform us not to women" (IV, ii, 35-36). The transformation here is no more a sign of effeminacy than Antony's wearing of Cleopatra tires and mantles. He is merely commenting that tears are womanly as he has done earlier in the play after Fulvia's death is reported. Then as now he explains that soldiers cannot cry, that "indeed the tears live in an onion, that should water this sorrow" (I, ii, 167-168). This reversal of roles, moreover, is paralleled and contrasted by many other characters in the play. Octavia's total and cloying passivity is contrasted with Cleopatra's "activity". Charmian is and shall be more "beloving than belov'd" (I, ii, 22), and Mardian thinks not what Mars did with Venus, but "What Venus did with Mars" (I, v, 18)!

The problem of the confusion or of the blending of the sexes into one is but one of the questions of love raised by the play. Whether or not the sexes "blend" into a Platonic one or remain sovereign entities is a question raised, but not answered, in the play. The search for "the other half" is contrasted with the search for identity and sovereignty. Thus while Knight sees the play as melting toward a oneness, Danby sees the play as moving toward a merging and then falling apart.[101] Daiches stresses the search for identity to the exclusion of the search for union. The "meaning" of the play, he says, is "– to summarize it crudely – about the different roles that man can play on the various stages which human activity provides for him, and about the relation of these roles to the player's true identity".[102] Lenora Leet, who characterizes the play as one of Worldly Love, would agree with Daiches in her explanation of the supposed infidelity of the lovers:

The mode of infidelity, of which Antony and Cleopatra have both been guilty, is, however, common only to Worldly Love. It is the infidelity to love caused by fidelity to self. Worldly lovers are sovereign beings who do not wish to lose themselves but to find another. They do not desire to achieve union but to remain "such a twain" a "mutual pair."[103]

101 Danby, p. 140.
102 Daiches, p. 344.
103 Leet, p. 302.

Miss Leet, like Mr. Daiches, sees this search for identity or sovereignty (as opposed to submission to Caesar, lover, or Fortune) as central to the play:

But Antony does not choose to die simply because his love for Cleopatra does not permit him to outlive her. His love had been fulfilled in life, and death can assure it no greater truth or fulfillment. No, he must die for the same reason that he believes Cleopatra has, and, in fact, shortly will die, because their sovereignty has been defeated.[104]

The evidence for such an interpretation is strong in the play. Antony indeed does state at Cleopatra's reported death that she "by her death our Caesar tells/ 'I am conqueror of myself' " (IV, xiv, 61-62). His own last words cry out his sovereignty:

> the greatest prince o' the world,
> The noblest; and do now not basely die,
> Not cowardly put off my helmet to
> My countryman: a Roman, by a Roman
> Valiantly vanquish'd.
>
> (IV, xv, 54-58)

The worry of losing his sovereign self is always with him. He tells Octavia that

> If I lose mine honour,
> I lose myself: better I were not yours
> Than yours so branchless.
>
> (III, iv, 22-24)

After he literally and symbolically follows Cleopatra's retreat, he bemoans the fact that he has "lost command" (III, xi, 23). He asks her whither she has led him (l. 51), acknowledging her as his "conqueror" (l. 66):

> Thy full supremacy thou knew'st, and that
> Thy beck might from the bidding of the gods
> Command me.
>
> (ll. 59-61)

Antony often speaks of himself and Cleopatra as distinct objects. He speaks, for example, of "An Antony" (IV, ii, 18) and Cleopatra seems to be striving to catch "another Antony" (V, ii, 345)

[104]   *Ibid.*, p. 309.

in her strong toil of grace. In her first appearance with Antony on stage Cleopatra says, "I'll seem the fool I am not; Antony/ Will be himself" (I, i, 42-43), to which Antony responds, "But stirr'd by Cleopatra". Thus they remain separate but united, like the lovers in Donne's "A Valediction: forbidding mourning": [105]

> Our separation so abides and flies,
> That thou, residing here, goes yet with me;
> And I, hence fleeting, here remain with thee.
>   (I, iii, 102-104)

Leone Ebreo's Philo can thus introduce the idea that lovers are "Only one, or else four".[106] Sophia then says, "That two people may be one, I can understand, since all lovers are united and become one in love; but how can they be four?" Philo's explanation is short and clear: "Each one being transformed into the other becomes two, at once both lover and beloved; and two multiplied by two makes four, so that each of them is twain, and both together are one and four." [107] Thus while *Antony and Cleopatra*, like Sonnets 42, 62, and 133, alludes to the Platonic One, as in the confusion of the sexes in the play, there is also present the idea of one love with two distinct people (cf. Sonnets 36 and 39).

Just what composes "An Antony" is a question answered only by the entire play. Philo, in the opening scene, feels that the Antony who loves Cleopatra is not only less than the Roman Antony, but unworthy even of being called Antony:

> Sir, sometimes, when he is not Antony,
> He comes too short of that great property
> Which still should go with Antony.
>   (ll. 57-59)

---

[105] John Donne, "A Valediction: forbidding mourning", in *Poems*, ed. Herbert J. C. Grierson (London, Oxford University Press, 1912), ll. 21-24:
> Our two soules therefore, which are one,
>   Though I must goe, endure not yet
> A breach, but an expansion,
>   Like gold to ayery thinnesse beate.

All quotations from Donne in this work are from this edition of his poems.
[106] Leone Ebreo, p. 260.
[107] *Ibid.*, Cf. Castiglione, p. 315.

The lines of Philo neither contradict, nor correct either Cleopatra's, Dolabella's, Caesar's, or our own view of Antony. The
interaction of all these raises the question in the play. Only the
play provides the answer.

The separate identity or sovereignty of two such "peerless" (I,
i, 40) beings is emphasized from the very meeting of the already
world-renowned individuals. Their meeting is more a competition
than union, for Cleopatra clearly defies Antony's hitherto un-
challenged sovereignty by her entrance:

> The city cast
> Her people out upon her; and Antony,
> Enthron'd i' the market-place, did sit alone,
> Whistling to the air; which, but for vacancy,
> Had gone to gaze on Cleopatra too,
> And made a gap in nature.
>
> (II, ii, 213-218)

After the union of the lovers, Cleopatra is as worried at the
possibility of losing her identity as Antony is. "O, my oblivion
is a very Antony,/ And I am all forgotten" (I, iii, 90-91), she
complains. Her concern, then, is for her "self", not for Antony.
Antony's concern for self, which we have noted, later becomes
an obsession with him. When Thidias fails to respond to Antony
as he did to the Antony of old, he cries, "Have you no ears?/ I
am Antony yet" (III, xiii, 92-93). Not only does Antony assert
his own identity; he makes clear that Cleopatra has lost hers. It
it with clear contempt and jealousy that he speaks "of she here,
– what's her name,/ Since she was Cleopatra" (ll. 98-99). Whatever she is now, he is certain she is no longer the Cleopatra he
loved. But once his jealous rage is over and he is "satisfied" (l.
167), Cleopatra says, "Since my lord/ Is Antony again, I will be
Cleopatra" (ll. 186-187). This identity of Antony seems the point
of Enobarbus' discussion at the opening of II, ii and that between
Agrippa and Enobarbus in III, ii (ll. 6 ff.).

Yet while Antony's uniqueness as "the Arabian bird" (III, ii,
12) stresses his individual sovereignty, his union with Cleopatra
is also stressed in the play. In addition to his wearing her tires
and mantles and her wearing his sword, the confusion occurs

again in I, ii, for example, when Cleopatra enters and Enobarbus comments "Hush, here comes Antony." The fact that Charmian responds, "Not he, the queen" (l. 76), despite the fact that Ridley "corrects" the Folio reading in which the stage direction "*Enter* CLEOPATRA" comes before Enobarbus' line instead of after it. Thus the search for both individuality and union in love is dramatized in the play.

When Antony cries that he is Antony yet (III, xiii), however, some critics have seen more jealousy than a search for identity. Lloyd, for example, argues that the jealous rages of both the protagonists are such that they are enough to deny the name of love to their relationship.[108] Cleopatra is jealous not only of Octavia (II, v) but of the dead Iras as well, who may "first meet the curled Antony". Neither does she trust Antony with Iras, for she fears he will "make demand of her, and spend that kiss/ Which is my heaven to have" (V, ii, 300-302). The context of the scene, however, argues more for the totality of Cleopatra's love than for her supposedly selfish jealousy. Her very death argues for sovereignty from Caesar and Fortune – but not from Antony, whom she is joining. Her jealousy contrasts with the behavior of Octavia and is a part of her Art with Antony. She is constantly a challenge to him, for he can never take her for granted. Indeed, her angry jealousy is an incentive to love. Capellanus in his chapter on "How Love, Once Consummated, May be Increased", declares:

Love increases, too, if one of the loves shows he is angry at the other; for the lover falls at once into a great fear that this feeling which has arisen in his beloved may last forever. Love increases, likewise, if one of the lovers feels real jealousy, which is called, in fact, the nurse of love.[109]

Indeed, the God of Love himself says flatly in his Second Rule of Love: "He who is not jealous cannot love." [110] Rule Twenty-One underscores the idea by stating that "Real jealousy always increases the feeling of love", while Rule Three seems to ad-

---

[108]   Lloyd, p. 89.
[109]   Capellanus, p. 27. .
[110]   *Ibid.*, p. 42.

monish Octavia for the lack of totality of her love: "No one can be bound by a double love." The importance of jealousy in considerations of love is reflected by the repetition and length of its consideration in Burton's anatomy of "the lover's melancholy".[111] But no background of jealousy in love is necessary to understand the jealous anger that provokes Cleopatra to threaten Charmian for comparing Caesar with Antony (I, v, 66 ff.). Juliet makes a similar threat to the Nurse in wishing her tongue be blistered (III, ii, 90) for wishing shame on Romeo (even though he has just killed her beloved kinsman, Tybalt). That jealousy need not be pejorative is reflected in Rosalind's declaration to Orlando that "I will be more jealous of thee than a Barbary cock-pigeon over his hen" (*As You Like It,* IV, i, 150-151). That jealousy is a part of even the most noble who love is clear to all who have read or seen *Othello*.

Another aspect of love often discussed in Renaissance and classical discussions of love and in *Antony and Cleopatra* as well is the idea "that the eyes are a guide in love".[112] Indeed, they are often characterized as the "trustie messengers that may carrie the ambassades of the hart".[113] The reasons given are explicit:

Because they often times declare with a more force what passiō there is inwardly, than can the tongue, or letters, or messages, so that they not onely disclose the thoughtes, but also manie times kindle love in the hart of the person beloved. For those lively spirits that issue out at the eyes, because they are levelled at, like a shaft to the pricke, naturally pearce to the hart, as to their resting place and there are at rest with those other spirits: and with the most subtill and fine nature of bloud which they carire with them, infect the bloude about the hart, where they come to, and warme it: and make it like unto themselves, and apt to receive the imprinting of the image, which they have carried away with them. Wherefore by litle and comming and going the way through the eyes to the hart, and bring backe with them the tunder and striking yron of beautie and grace, these messengers kindle with the puffing of desire the fire that so burneth, and never ceaseth consuming, for alwaies they bring some matter of hope to nourish it.[114]

---

[111]   Burton, III, 18, 130-131, 166, 295-357.
[112]   Castiglione, p. 247.
[113]   *Ibid.*, p. 246.
[114]   *Ibid.*, pp. 246-247.

While the eyes note the sensual and physical beauty, "the eyes of the mind",[115] which are "the windows of the soul",[116] note the spiritual qualities of the beloved as well.[117]

The significance of the eyes in *Antony and Cleopatra* is heralded from the second line of the play, when we hear that Antony's

> **goodly eyes**
> That o'er the files and musters of the war
> Have glow'd like plated Mars, now bend, now turn
> The office and devotion of their view
> Upon a tawny front. . . .
>
> (I, i, 2-6)

The eyes of Antony that turn their "devotion" toward Cleopatra are loving eyes and differ from the eyes of wisdom and reason in the eye-motif in *Lear*. Cleopatra as an artist of love knows well the importance of eyes in love, so that in her first appearance to Antony in her barge, her gentlewomen "tended her i' the eyes,/ And made their bends adorning" (II, ii, 207-208). The physical eyes of Antony are those which "eat" Cleopatra, and Cleopatra only (II, ii, 226). It is precisely because in Antony's jealous view Cleopatra's eyes are not for him alone, however, that he asks his jealously rhetorical question: "To flatter Caesar, would you mingle eyes/ With one that ties his points?" (III, xiii, 156-157).

But if it is the eyes that recognize "the other half", it is equally "true" that love is blind and unreasonable. The blindness of the Renaissance Cupid (not so in classical art and only rarely so in classical literature) [118] most obviously attests to this belief. But the blindness of Cupid is not mentioned in the play – perhaps because

---

[115]   *Ibid.*, p. 318. Cf. *Hamlet* (I, ii, 185): "in my mind's eye".

[116]   Burton, III, 102. Cf. Charmian to Cleopatra after the death of her mistress: "Downy windows, close,/ And golden Phoebus, never be beheld/ Of eyes again so royal!" (V, ii, 315-317).

[117]   Leone Ebreo, p. 212.

[118]   Erwin Panofsky, *Studies in Iconology. Humanistic Themes in the Art of the Renaissance* (New York, Harper and Row, 1962), p. 95. Cf. Blind Cupid in *Much Ado*, I, i, 256; *A Midsummer-Night's Dream*, I, i, 235; *King Lear*, IV, vi, 140-141; and Blind Love in *Two Gentlemen of Verona*, II, i, 76; Sonnet 137; and Burton, III, 178.

of the deliberateness and awareness of its experienced lovers. Indeed, the very openness of the love of Antony and Cleopatra attests its power. Maecenas' is shocked at the enthronement of the lovers in the market place "in the public eye" (III, vi, 11). Castiglione himself flatly declares that "An open love is too hard a matter." [119] His advice to the perfect Courtier is "to keep his loves secrete".[120] Capellanus' God of Love in Rule Thirteen agrees that "When made public love rarely endures." [121] But Capellanus also says that "Love increases, too, if it happens to last after it has been made public." [122] That Antony and Cleopatra's love survives this test proves its superiority to merely professed or hidden love.

The image of the lover is thus conveyed to his beloved through the eyes, and to the lover this image is all-important. Even after Egypt has led Antony to retreat, his concern is to avoid her seeing him so degraded:

> See,
> How I convey my shame out of thine eyes,
> By looking back what I have left behind
> Stroy'd in dishonour.
>
> (III, xi, 51-54)

This mutual concern for appearance, moreover, is seen in Cleopatra's declaration that "my becomings kill me, when they do not/ Eye well to you" (I, iii, 96-97). Indeed, totality of this concern is one of the aspects of the nature of love dramatized in the play. When Antony speaks to Caesar, as contrasted with his speeches to Cleopatra, he says "as nearly as I may,/ I'll play the penitent to you. But . . ." (II, ii, 91-92). There are no "buts" for lovers. The God of Love makes clear that "Love can deny nothing to love." [123] It knows no dimensions.[124] It is subject to any task, any toil.[125] Phaedrus in Plato's *Symposium* says that "the lover

---

[119]   Castiglione, p. 248.
[120]   *Ibid.*, p. 249.
[121]   Capellanus, p. 42.
[122]   *Ibid.*, p. 27.
[123]   *Ibid.*, p. 43.
[124]   *Burton*, III, 212.
[125]   *Ibid.*, III, 192.

on his part is ready to confer any favor that he rightly can on his gracious loving one, and the other is ready to yield any compliance that he rightly can to him who is to make him wise and good . . . ." [126] Shakespeare utilizes this law of love from his early *Venus and Adonis* when Venus in tears is told, "And one sweet kiss shall pay this countless debt" (l. 84), to *Antony and Cleopatra* when Antony similarly reassures Cleopatra:

> Fall not a tear, I say, one of them rates
> All that is won and lost: give me a kiss,
> Even this repays me.
> (III, xi, 69-71)

The extremity of the demands the beloved may make of her lover is reflected in Beatrice's emphatic demand to Benedick to prove his love for her: "Kill Claudio" (*Much Ado*, IV, i, 291). This law of love, moreover, is paralleled on the political level with Menas' offer to Pompey: "I am the man/ Will give thee all the world" (II, vii, 64-65). Pompey's response carries with it the capricious unbelief of Cleopatra's answer to Antony's similar offer. Pompey responds, "Has thou drunk well?" in a tone not unlike Cleopatra's "I'll set a bourn how far to be belov'd" (I, i, 16). Indeed, if Antony's love, like his dotage, is seen as that which "O'erflows the measure" (I, i, 2), the extremity is presented as a love superior to that of Octavia's, Caesar's, Ventidius', or even Enobarbus' reasoned love for him. Ventidius observes, "I have done enough" (III, i, 12), and unquestionably he has, yet his love is but a trifle to that boundless love which needs must find out "new heaven, new earth". Indeed, love is boundless, because it is constantly growing:

> Love is a babe; then might I not say so,
> To give full growth to that which still doth grow.[127]
> (Sonnet 115)

The love of all others in the play is petty when contrasted with that of Antony and Cleopatra, for "There's beggary in love that can be reckon'd" (I, i, 15).

---

126 Plato, p. 44.
127 Cf. Donne, "Loves growth" and "Loves infinitenesse".

There's beggary even in the love of friendship when contrasted with the love of man and woman, the play asserts, despite The Elizabethan Attitude that supposedly rated friendship higher. Even in the homosexually slanted *Symposium* this idea is introduced into the discussion of love. Phaedrus discusses the superiority of Alcestis' love for her husband to all other loves for him,

for she was willing to lay down her life on behalf of her husband, when no one else would, although he had a father and mother; but the tenderness of her love so far exceeded theirs that they seemed to be as strangers to their own son, having no concern with him; and so noble did this action of hers appear, not only to men but also to the gods, that among the many who have done virtuously she was one of the very few to whom the gods have granted the privilege of returning to earth, in admiration of her virtue; such exceeding honor is paid by them to the devotion and virtue of love.[128]

The totality of concern in love is also voiced by Ladie Emilia in *The Courtier:* "For if you did love, all your desires should bee to please the woman beloved, and to will the selfe same thing that she willeth, for this is the law of love." [129] This law of love is enacted in the play by Cleopatra's assertion that "I am quickly ill, and well,/ So Antony loves" (I, iii, 73-74) just as clearly as Octavia dramatizes the Third Law of Love in Capellanus: "No one can be bound by a double love." [130] This Octavia demonstrates when she tells us that her heart is "parted betwixt two friends" (III, vi, 77) and "neither way inclines" (III, ii, 50).

Indeed, Octavia often dramatizes in the play what is almost love, what is sometimes considered love, but what ultimately is not love, for "Love is not love/ Which alters when it alteration finds,/ Or bends with the remover to remove" (Sonnet 116).[131] The idea that the beloved is all, common in the Sonnets (91, 92, 109, and 112, for example), is a cliché of life and literature. It is

---

128 Plato, p. 37.
129 Castiglione, p. 245.
130 Capellanus, p. 42.
131 Cf. The King of France in *King Lear*: "Love's not love/ When it is mingled with regards that stands/ Aloof from th' entire point" (I, i, 241-243).

seen throughout the relationship of Antony and Cleopatra, as is the reservation that all this involves the gamble of making the beloved so powerful that the lover may lose all. Antony is well aware of the power he has given Cleopatra:

> Egypt, thou knew'st too well,
> My heart was to thy rudder tied by the strings,
> And thou shouldst tow me after. O'er my spirit
> Thy full supremacy thou knew'st, and that
> Thy beck might from the bidding of the gods
> Command me.
>
> (III, xi, 56-61)

The play, moreover, like Sonnet 116, is also concerned with what is not love. In addition to the love that alters not being love, love is not love which is not heterosexual. Unlike the *Symposium,* then, *Antony and Cleopatra* does not consider love between members of the same sex, love.[132] Like Capellanus, the play asserts that "in love you should note first of all that love cannot exist except between persons of opposite sexes".[133] The earth and water of the physical that is necessary to ascend to the fire and air of the spiritual is a theme we have noted at length in Chapter III. Cleopatra derides purely idealized love when she says, "As well a woman with a eunuch play'd,/ As with a woman" (II, v, 5-6). Although "good will" may "plead pardon", it comes punningly "too short" (ll. 8-9) of the "deeds" (I, v, 14-15) of love when combined with good will.

But if love has a physical basis, love is not merely physical. We have noted that it includes friendship, for example. Love, the play asserts, is not lust. Sonnet 129 contains the most famous conception of what has often been equated with Shakespeare's own idea of lust:

> Th' expense of spirit in a waste of shame
> Is lust in action; and till action, lust
> Is perjur'd, murd'rous, bloody, full of blame,
> Savage, extreme, rude, cruel, not to trust;
> Enjoy'd no sooner but despised straight,
> Past reason hunted, and no sooner had

132   Plato, pp. 39 ff.
133   Capellanus, p. 4.

> Past reason hated, as a swallow'd bait
> On purpose laid to make the taker mad;
> [Mad] in pursuit and in possession so;
> Had, having, and in quest to have, extreme;
> A bliss in proof, and [prov'd a] very woe;
> Before, a joy propos'd; behind, a dream.
>> All this the world well knows; yet none knows well
>> To shun the heaven that leads men to this hell.

The feelings of Antony and Cleopatra for each other after each hears of the death of the other (as well as the movement in tone of the play) argue against the purely physical attractiveness that leads to that hell. Indeed the cloylessness of Cleopatra's infinite variety argues against the hate that follows possession. The difference is voiced by Adonis who tells us that

> Love comforteth like sunshine after rain,
> But Lust's effect is tempest after sun;
> Love's gentle spring doth always fresh remain,
> Lust's winter comes ere summer half be done;
>> Love surfeits not, Lust like a glutton dies;
>> Love is all truth, Lust full of forged lies.
>>> (*Venus and Adonis*, ll. 799-804)

To the lustful, moreover, all objects of love are the same. The jealous exclusiveness of Antony and Cleopatra argues for their love. Capellanus speaks of the lack of discrimination in the lustful:

An excess of passion is a bar to love, because there are men who are slaves to such passionate desire that they cannot be held in the bonds of love – men who, after they have thought long about some woman or even enjoyed her, when they see another woman straightway desire her embraces, and they forget about the services they have received from their first love and they feel no gratitude for them. Men of this kind lust after every woman they see; their love is like that of a shameless dog.[134]

If lust demonstrates man's kinship to other animals, love, the play would assert, raises him from his dungy earth to fire and air.

But if the nature of love as discussed in the play includes fire and air, it is grounded in its base of earth and water. If it searches

---

[134] *Ibid.*, p. 5.

for a "new heaven", it also contains the hellish. Those critics who would have the entire play characterized by lust, decay, and evil argue that had Shakespeare "intended" to portray Cleopatra sympathetically,[135] he would have created her a blonde, for The Elizabethan Mind preferred fair to dark. Burton, for example, reminds us of Plato, who he says "saith [that] the fairer the object is, the more eagerly it is sought".[136] That Burton interprets "fairer" here as "blonder" is reflected in the length at which he discusses the yellow hair [137] and black eyes [138] of The Ideal Beauty. In fact yellow hair was looked on with great favor, "which belike makes our *Venetian* Ladies at this day to counterfeit yellow hair so much . . . ." [139] But this does not prevent Burton, born in Elizabethan's reign after all, from acknowledging (as Elizabethan scholars often do not) that Cleopatra was beautiful.[140] Indeed, perhaps a blonde was Antony's Ideal Love. But if so, that love is as unreal as his love for Octavia when contrasted with his real and dramatized love for the dark Egyptian Queen, pinched black by Phoebus' amorous kisses. This difference between the real and the ideal is the subject of Sonnet 130:

> My mistress' eyes are nothing like the sun
> Coral is far more red than her lips' red;
> If snow be white, why then her breasts are dun;
> If hairs be wires, black wires grow on her head.

No defense of dark beauty is more eloquent than Sonnet 127:

> In the old age black was not counted fair,
> Or if it were, it bore not beauty's name;
> But now is black beauty's successive heir,
> And beauty slander'd with a bastard shame:
> For since each hand hath put on Nature's power,
> Fairing the foul with Art's false borrow'd face,
> Sweet beauty hath no name, no holy bower,
> But is profan'd, if not lives in disgrace.

---

[135] See discussion, Chapter II.
[136] Burton, III, 11.
[137] *Ibid.*, III, 91-92.
[138] *Ibid.*, III, 95.
[139] *Ibid.*, III, 91-92.
[140] *Ibid.*, III, 179.

> Therefore my mistress' [brows] are raven black,
> Her eyes so suited, and they mourners seem
> At such who, not born fair, no beauty lack,
> Sland'ring creation with a false esteem:
>> Yet so they mourn, becoming of their woe,
>> That every tongue says beauty should look so.

The idea that black is fair to the lover is an important motif in the Sonnets. In Sonnet 131, for example, the lover tells his dark lady that "to my dear doting heart/ Thou art the fairest and most precious jewel" and that "Thy black is fairest in my judgement's place". This feeling reaches its ecstatic, hyperbolic peak in Sonnet 132, when the lover declares

> > > black
> Then will I swear beauty herself is
> And all they foul that thy complexion lack.

Neither does the equal vehemency of his "retraction" in Sonnet 147 negate his love for his dark lady. While he now explains,

> I have sworn thee fair and thought thee bright,
> Who art as black as hell, as dark as night,

the "reversal" rather illustrates the extremities of love than a negation of his former "illusion". While Antony similarly cries out against his "Triple-turn'd whore" (IV, xii, 13), he does so because of his love-founded jealousy.[141] Just as the last line of the Sonnets ("Love's fire heats water, water cools not love", Sonnet 154), so do Antony's dying words (IV, xv, 45 ff.) bespeak undying love. Since it is a dramatic tradition to regard the words of a dying protagonist to be as true as those of his soliloquies, we can hardly doubt his love.

Although G. Wilson Knight, we have seen, argues that "all evil is resolved in the whole", the question of love's good and evil is one raised dramatically in the play. The good or evil nature of love is one characteristically discussed in love treatises. Plato's *Symposium*, for example, considers the subject at length.[142] Capellanus notes that "Many are the evils of love", and then continues

---

[141]   See discussion of love and jealousy above.
[142]   Plato, pp. 67 ff.

to elaborate upon these evils.[143] Burton's discussion of love-melancholy considers the problem in a reference to Plotinus: "*It is worth the labour, saith, Plotinus, to consider well of Love, whether it be a God or a Devil or passion of the mind, or partly God, party Devil, partly passion.*" [144] Burton then discusses the opinions of Plato and Aristotle concerning the good and evil of love. Burton points out from Polybius that indeed "the heaven itself is said to be fair or foul . . . ." [145] Castiglione even castigates those "fonde persons, because they would have all goodnesse in the world without any ill, which is unpossible".[146] The impossibility of perfection was clear even to the young Shakespeare, who wrote in *The Rape of Lucrece*:

> But no perfection is so absolute,
> That some impurity doth not pollute.
>   (ll. 853-854)

The impossibility, perhaps even undesirability, of perfection is discussed in Sonnet 130, when the lover tells us that his beloved is no perfect goddess, but a human creature who "treads on the ground". The bad as well as the good compose love, both the play and the Sonnets agree:

> Roses have thorns, and silver fountains mud;
> Clouds and eclipses stain both moon and sun
> And loathsome canker lives in sweetest bud.
>   (Sonnet 35)

The lack of reason that we have discussed as an aspect of the nature of love, moreover, makes the imperfect seem perfect in the beloved: "Take mine eyes", says Burton's "love-sick spectator Nicomacus", and

thou wilt think she is a Goddess, dote on her forthwith, count all her vices, virtues; her imperfections, informities, absolute and perfect. If she be flat-nosed, she is lovely; if hook-nosed, kingly; if dwarfish and little, pretty; if tall, proper and man-like, our brave British *Boadicea*;

143   Capellanus, pp. 46 ff.
144   Burton, III, 10.
145   *Ibid.*
146   Castiglione, p. 89.

if crooked, wise; if monstrous, comely; her defects are no defects at all, she hath no deformities.[147]

Donne is but one poet who writes of "Loves Alchymie". Cleopatra herself, like the beloved that "mak'st faulst graces" (Sonnet 96), makes "defect perfection" (II, ii, 231) – even to the cynical Enobarbus. Part of the infinite variety of love, the play would argue, is that it comprises evil as well as good. It is part of the cloylessness of Cleopatra. Ovid in "The Art of Love" tells of the boredom that accompanies perfect goodness:

> Sweetness we cannot stand: refresh us with juice that is
> bitter.
> Often a boat goes down by a favoring wind.
> That is what keeps some wives from being loved by their
> husbands.
> It's all too easy for him, coming whenever he will.
> (III, 581-584)

The best answer to those who condemn the relationship of Antony and Cleopatra as totally evil is that of Sonnet 121:

> 'Tis better to be vile than vile esteemed
> When not to be receives reproach of being,
> And the just pleasure lost which is so deemed
> Not by our feeling but by others' seeing.
> For why should others' false adulterate eyes
> Give salutation to my sportive blood?
> Or on my frailties why are frailer spies,
> Which in their wills count bad what I think good?
> No, I am that I am, and they that level
> At my abuses reckon up their own;
> I may be straight, though they themselves be bevel;
> By their rank thoughts my deeds must not be shown, –
>   Unless this general evil they maintain:
>   All men are bad, and in their badness reign.

While the questions of Fortune, Fate, and Free Will are ones raised in virtually all of Shakespeare's plays, the questions here are focused on their relation to love. It is Fortuna, not Octavia, who is Cleopatra's real rival and whom she must overcome to shackle accident and bolt up change. While Fortuna is but a

[147]   Burton, III, 182.

"false huswife" (IV, xv, 44) to her erstwhile favorite, Cleopatra remains faithful to Antony, for "her fortunes mingled" with his entirely (IV, xiv, 24). Fortuna's love is false since "Love's not Time's fool" (Sonnet 116), and she vacillates in her love, indeed preferring Octavius (II, iii, 15-29). Antony, like Romeo, proves to be "fortune's fool" (*Romeo and Juliet*, III, i, 141), not Cleopatra's. Even Pompey realizes that Fortune's love allows no sovereignty. She merely conquers:

> Well, I know not
> What counts harsh fortune casts upon my face,
> But in my bosom shall she never come,
> To make my heart her vassal.
> (II, vi, 53-56)

But Fortune's hold over Antony is strong. While Antony is aware that "Fortune knows,/ We scorn her most when most she offers blows" (III, xi, 73-74), his concern with his glorious past when he knew not Cleopatra, when he "With half the bulk o' the world play'd as I pleas'd,/ Making and marring fortunes" (ll. 64-65), is one that is difficult to put aside. It is not until IV, xii, that he is able to say, "Fortune and Antony part here" (l. 19). Indeed, until then Antony has followed his own advice to Caesar and been "a child o' the time" (II, vii, 99) and "married but his occasion" (II, vi, 128). Cleopatra is also late in her discovery that to be merely a child of Time is "paltry" and to be subject to Fortune is to be but "fortune's knave" (V, ii, 2 ff.). But the question of whether Antony and Cleopatra were destined to love, whether they were star-crossed or self-crossed, is a question left to the audience. Fortune is a complex concept in the play, comprising free will within her confines, for "men's judgements are/ A parcel of their fortunes" (III, xiii, 31-32). Only love by a loving death can shackle accidents and bolt up change (V, ii, 5). The idea is one found in the Sonnets as well:

> So shalt thou feed on Death that feeds on men,
> And Death once dead there's no more dying then.
> (Sonnet 146)

Unlike Marvell's most famous love poem, then, *Antony and Cleopatra* suggests that through love we can make our sun stand still.[148] A contrast is made in the play not only between Pompey (who is offered the chance to be "lord of the whole world" and refuses) but with Caesar, who gains the whole world, only to be Fortune's knave. If Caesar at the end of the play has the whole world and Antony dies, Caesar still is not the hero of the play. He is as foolish as Emilia, who would be unfaithful "for all the world" (*Othello*, IV, ii, 68 ff.), while Antony at the end of the play rises as high as Desdemona in his death. The "full-fortun'd Caesar" (IV, xv, 24) remains her knave, and Octavia merely "a blessed lottery" (II, ii, 243).

Whatever the nature of love, the play asserts, whether sublime, holy, degrading, or merely comic – or all of these – there is something unreasonable, inexplicable, even magical in its essence. Hermia's father, like Desdemona's, bemoans the use of enchantments in securing love. A discussion of magic appears in Castiglione's,[149] Burton's,[150] and Ficino's [151] considerations of the nature of love. Love's mystery or magic is all that can explain the inexplicable. It is, after all, a divine madness. The inexplicable quality of the magic of love is dramatized, as we have seen, in the image of the crocodile, "shap'd, sir, like itself, and it is as broad as it hath breadth: it is just as high as it is, and moves with it own organs. It lives by that which nourisheth it, and the elements once out of it, it transmigrates" (II, vii, 41-45). Its inexplicable nature is both the cause and effect of Cleopatra's speech in I, iii:

> Courteous lord, one word:
> Sir, you and I must part, but that's not it:
> Sir, you and I have lov'd, but there's not it;
> That you know well, something it is I would, –
> (ll. 86-89)

The nature of love, like Antony's very being, is as "indistinct/

---

[148]   Cf. Andrew Marvell, "To his Coy Mistress", in *Poems*, ed. H. M. Margoliouth (Oxford, Clarendon Press, 1927), ll. 45-46:
> Thus, though we cannot make our Sun
> Stand still, yet we will make him run.
[149]   Castiglione, p. 101.
[150]   Burton, III, 96 and 157.
[151]   Ficino, p. 221.

As water is in water" (IV, xiv, 10-11), as changing as the cloud that characterizes his essence (IV, xiv, 2-14). However, magical and mysterious the nature of love, the movement and tone of the play would argue (like Plato's Diotima) that "the mystery of man and woman" is "a divine thing, for conception and generation are a principle of immortality in the mortal creature." [152]

The point of the many parallels in Plato, Ovid, Burton, Capellanus, Ficino, and Shakespeare's other works that focus on love, is not that he is indebted to any of them as sources, nor that the ideas of love in the play are "typically Elizabethan". The point is that *Antony and Cleopatra* considers many of the same subjects as do other Renaissance treatments of the nature of love. It is not, as most critics have contended,[153] merely a dazzling but ultimately empty play. Shakespeare's play is as full and deep a treatment of the nature and paradoxes of love as any ever written. It differs only because it "seems to enact its meaning, to do and to give rather than to talk about . . .".[154]

[152] Plato, p. 73.
[153] See discussion, Chapter I.
[154] Leavis, p. 160.

V

THE QUESTION OF LOVE AND THE LOVE-ACT: SOME SUGGESTIONS ABOUT STRUCTURE

If critics have agreed on little else than the dazzling superficiality of *Antony and Cleopatra*,[1] that little must include the observation that its structure is "loose". The critical observation is hardly new. Samuel Johnson states flatly that there is neither craftsmanship nor art in the structure of the play: "The events, of which the principal are described according to history, are produced without any art of connection or care of disposition."[2] Undoubtedly the most influential denunciation of the artless structure of the play is that of A. C. Bradley. In *Shakespearean Tragedy* he makes clear his reason for omitting any analysis of *Antony and Cleopatra* from those of the four great tragedies. His reason is that it is "the most faultily constructed of all the tragedies".[3] While other critics have merely echoed his criticism of the structure without analysis, Bradley, though briefly, at least attempts to give some specific reasons for his observation. In his *Oxford Lectures on Poetry* in which that analysis appears, he sets forth his reasons for the opinion that the structure is faulty. "It is, no doubt", he says, "in the third and fourth Acts, very defective in construction."[4] He later elaborates that this defectiveness is owing to the lack of drama and action of the other plays:

In the first three Acts of our play what is there resembling this? Almost nothing. People converse, discuss, accuse one another, excuse themselves, mock, describe, drink together, arrange a marriage, meet

---

[1] See discussion, Chapter I.
[2] Johnson, X, 213.
[3] Bradley, *Shakespearean Tragedy*, p. 260.
[4] Bradley, *Oxford Lectures*, pp. 282-283.

and part; but they do not kill, do not even tremble or weep. . . . the
scenes we remember first are the least indispensable to the plot. One
at least is not essential to it at all. And this, the astonishing scene
where she storms at the messenger, strikes him, and draws her dagger
on him, is the one passage in the first half of the drama that contains
either an explosion of passion or an exciting bodily action.[5]

The whole first half of the play he sees as "amusing" but not
tragic.[6] Only in Act V does Cleopatra become "unquestionably
a tragic character, but, it appears to me, not till then".[7] The
structure that Bradley sees as "defective" soon becomes clear by
his "analysis". His view of the play, like that of Madeleine Doran,
is one which Miss Doran calls "the rise-and-fall pattern". The
view of Bradley and Miss Doran of the structure is, of course,
the rise and fall of Antony.[8]

Oliver Emerson speaks for the majority of critics when he
says, "The dramatic movement of the play is the ruin of Antony
under the stress of sensual passion . . .".[9] Ralph Behrens speaks
of the inadequacy of such a view of the play when he says, "If
Shakespeare had intended his audience to be concerned only with
the effect of that love on Antony, the play would have ended with
Antony's death in Act IV. From structural evidence, then, we
must conclude that Cleopatra is needed to demonstrate an important half of the major thesis of the play." [10]

Still viewing the play as "the story of Antony", J. Dover Wilson, with characteristic ingenuity, explains the fifth Act in this
manner:

But it is also Cleopatra's tragedy; she too must find her true greatness
and be touched to finest issues. This is the theme of Shakespeare's
fifth act, which is response to the challenge of the source; for when
the memoirs of the physician Olympus fell into Plutarch's hands he
was led to add a postscript to his *Life of Antony* which supplied the
dramatist with matter that could not be fitted into the normal tragic
scheme, and was yet of such surpassing interest and beauty as to

5   *Ibid.*, p. 284.
6   *Ibid.*, pp. 284-285.
7   *Ibid.*, p. 299. Cf. Craig, p. 268.
8   See discussion, Chapter II.
9   Emerson, p. 126.
10   Behrens, p. 37.

compel incorporation. Thus Shakespeare was driven to compose a
coda to the tragedy of Antony which many consider the most wonderful movement in any of his great symphonies.[11]

Despite his appended qualification, "Nor is the last act merely a
second catastrophe with Cleopatra as protagonist",[12] this *coda*, in
his view, is precisely that. The last act is somehow separate. As
in Bradley's view, Cleopatra does not figure strongly in the
"tragedy" until the fifth Act.

Since many critics, like Lloyd, have aptly pointed out that "if
we see Antony's tragedy as the centrepiece of the play, its structure is faulty",[13] some critics lacking Wilson's ingenuity have
searched for other "solutions" to explain the structure of the
play in terms of their preconceived notions of Shakespearean
Tragedy. Irving Ribner, for example, in *Patterns of Shakespearean
Tragedy*, attempts to squeeze *Antony and Cleopatra* into his preconceived pattern of Shakespearean character-tragedy:

> *Antony and Cleopatra* is two plays in one. For four acts it is a por-
> trait of a great man's self-destruction through devotion to a sin which
> is itself heroic and magnificent. In the fifth act it is a portrait of a
> great queen's awareness of sinful lust, her casting it off, and her
> dedication of herself instead to a love to which her death is a sacrifice
> in expiation for former sins.[14]

Thus *Antony and Cleopatra* has been considered loose and faulty
in structure chiefly by those who view the play as structured by
the rise and fall of Antony – those critics who would have all
Shakespeare's tragedies characterized by the rise and fall of a
noble man through a tragic flaw.[15] These critics would be able
to ignore any suggestion to the contrary (as they can with *Lear*

---

[11] Wilson, p. xxxii.
[12] *Ibid.*
[13] Lloyd, p. 94.
[14] Irving Ribner, *Patterns in Shakespearian Tragedy* (London, Methuen
and Co., 1960), p. 172. Cf. Craig, p. 280.
[15] See discussion in Chapter II. Thomas B. Stroup in "The Structure of
Antony and Cleopatra" in *Shakespeare Quarterly*, XV (Spring, 1964), says
that the play is both "a Gothic play" and one of Polonius' "tragical-
historical" plays (p. 290). Rather than seeing any real unity in the play,
however, he explains (or rationalizes) that "what was represented on the
stage must take its proper shape from the world's vast unity (p. 291).

and *Macbeth,* for example) except for the death of Antony in Act
IV and the fact that the play is nominally and integrally about
Cleopatra as well – in the first four acts as well as in the fifth.[16]
Still (with this rise-and-fall- pattern in mind) the structure of the
play is condemned by Craig as "not . . . carefully planned",[17] by
Waith as "the most episodic of the plays,[18] by Miss Doran as
"extensive and loose",[19] and by Charlton as "ultra-romantic" as
opposed to the "almost classical formality of *Coriolanus*".[20]
Aristotle provides the best answer to those who see unity only in
a single character:

A plot is not unified, as some think, because it is concerned with one
man, for a countless number of things happen to one man, some of
which cannot be combined with others in a single unit; thus there are
many acts by one man which cannot form parts of a unified action.[21]

Many of the charges, then, of defective and loose structure in
Antony and Cleopatra stem from a preference for the "classical"
formality of a play like *Coriolanus*. While Charlton merely labels
the structure of the play as "ultra-romantic", with the assumption
that all understand its meanings, all that seems clear is that he,
like many others who see *Antony and Cleopatra* as defective,
feels that all beauty is simplicity. Indeed, the contrast between
the simplicity and unity of Greek Drama and the ornamentation
of that of the Elizabethans has often been made, perhaps never
so well as by Coleridge:

Having intimated that times and manners lend their form and pres-
sure to the genius, it may be useful to draw a slight parallel between
the *ancient* and *modern stage*, as it existed in Greece and in England.
The Greeks were polytheists, their religion was local, the object of
all their knowledge, science, and taste, was their gods; their productions were therefore (if the expression may be allowed), *statuesque*.

16 See discussion of Cleopatra's roles in the imagery and themes, Chapters III and IV.
17 Craig, p. 268.
18 Eugene M. Waith, *The Herculean Hero in Marlowe, Chapman, Shakespeare, and Dryden* (London, Chatto and Windus, 1962), p. 121.
19 Madeleine Doran, *Endeavors of Art: A Study of Form in Elizabethan
Drama* (Madison, Wisconsin, University Press, 1954), p. 297.
20 Charlton, p. 15.
21 Aristotle, p. 80.

The moderns we may designate as *picturesque*; the end, complete harmony. The Greeks reared a structure, which, in its parts and as a whole, filled the mind with the calm and elevated impression of perfect beauty and symmetrical proportion. The moderns, blending materials, produced one striking whole. This may be illustrated by comparing the Pantheon with York Minster or Westminster Abbey. Upon the same scale we may compare Sophocles with Shakespeare: in the one there is a completeness, a satisfying, an excellence, on which mind can rest; in the other we see a blended multitude of materials, great and little, magnificent and mean, mingled, if we may so say, with a dissatisfying, or falling short of perfection, yet so promising of our progression, that we would not exchange it for that repose of the mind which dwells on the forms of symmetry in acquiescent admiration of grace. This general characteristic of the ancient and modern poetry might be exemplified in a parallel of their ancient and modern music: the ancient music consisted of melody by the succession of pleasing sounds; the modern embraces harmony, the result of combination and effect of the whole.[22]

The difference between contemporary architecture and a baroque church makes the contrast all the more clear. While functionalism and simplicity are key concepts in modern architecture, baroque architecture can hardly be termed less unified in structure because it is ornamented. This love of ornament in Elizabethan England extended not only to the clothing of the nobility (to a degree that we might consider excessive) but to poetry as well. The "confusion of Poetry and Rhetoric was, however, no peculiar vice of the Elizabethans. It goes back to Greek antiquity and the Roman, coarser-grained than the Greek, inevitably responded more heartily to Rhetoric than to Poetry." [23] Thus Plato's declaration that "when the ideas of the poet are stripped of the colors of poetry, you know, I think how they appear",[24] was echoed more vehemently in Du Bellay's exhaltation of "ornemens, sans lesquel toute oraison et poëme sont nuds, manques et debiles".[25] Indeed, the

---

[22]   Coleridge, II, 262-263. The comparisons made here by Coleridge, Raysor tells us, are ultimately based on Schlegel, *Werke*, 9-17. Cf. Kitto, pp. 209-210.

[23]   Willcock and Walker, p. lxxiv.

[24]   Plato, "The Republic", trans. Allan H. Gilbert in *Literary Criticism*, p. 48. Cf. Aristotle, p. 101.

[25]   Joachim Du Bellay, "La Défense et Illustration de la Langue Française", in *Œuvres Complètes* (Paris, Revue de la Renaissance, 1903), I, 11.

very word "ornament" in the Renaissance was "partly or wholly synonymous with delight. It represents the dualism of the didactic theory of poetry, the poet must select good ideas and ornament them properly." [26] Perhaps the most clear and concise statement of this dualistic theory of poetry is that of the greatest poet of the seventeenth-century, John Milton:

> I thought, therefore, that if it were the will of God those men should perform such gallant exploits, it must be likewise his will, that when performed, there should be others to set them forth with becoming dignity and ornament: and that the truth, after being defended by arms, should be alike defended by reason – the only defense which is truly and properly human.[27]

If abundant, however, the use of ornament was not to be flagrant. Puttenham proclaimed it "a great fault to vse figuratiue speaches foolishly and indiscreetly," [28] while Sidney likened such excess to the capricious casting of "sugar and spice upon every dish that is served to the table." [29]

Still critics, viewing *Antony and Cleopatra* more as a functional contemporary building or one with the simplicity of the Pantheon than as a baroque church, have deplored its "defective expansiveness and ornamentation." Bradley, for example, clearly utilizes this contrast in his "analysis" of "Shakespeare as Artist" in his *Shakespearean Tragedy:*

> To come then to real defects, (a) one may be found in places where Shakespeare strings together a number of scenes, some very short, in which the *dramatis personae* are frequently changed; as though a novelist were to tell his story in a succession of short chapters, in which he flitted from one group of his characters to another. This method shows itself here and there in the pure tragedies (e.g. in the last Act of *Macbeth*), but it appears most decidedly where the historical material was undramatic, as in the middle part of *Antony and Cleopatra.*[30]

[26] Gilbert, p. 674n. For Puttenham on ornament, see pp. 3, 137, 138-139, 298.
[27] John Milton, "A Second Defense" in *Works,* ed. Frank Allen Patterson *et al.* (New York, Columbia University Press, 1931), VIII, 11.
[28] Puttenham, p. 8.
[29] Sir Philip Sidney, "A Defense of Poetry", in *Literary Criticism*, p. 454.
[30] Bradley, *Shakespearean Tragedy*, p. 71.

The defectiveness of the flitting that Bradley sees in Acts III and IV obviously arises from his analogy of chapters with scenes. While there are thirteen scenes in Act III of the New Arden edition of the play and fifteen in Act IV, he can hardly view the structure as "loose" because of the many scenes in the acts. In the First Folio the only act and scene division is the *Actus Primus. Scaena Prima.* that begins the play. In the continuous performance of an Elizabethan production, there would be no awareness of acts and scenes any more than there is in a Shakespearean performance today. The *reductio ad absurdum* of the structural ramifications of Acts in Shakespeare is the absurd (but hardly reduced) volume of T. W. Baldwin.[31] The act divisions are the business of the editor, not of the critic or spectator.

If the rise and fall of a single character in a scheme determined by the five-act structure does not describe the construction of *Antony and Cleopatra*, however, there have been few other descriptions of the structure of the play to look to as an alternative. Yet the terms "form" and "structure" are ubiquitous in modern criticism. René Wellek states that it would be so "easy to collect hundreds of definitions of 'form' and 'structure' from contemporary critics and aestheticians and to show that they contradict each other so radically and basically that it may be best to abandon the terms".[32] Part of this confusion at least he attributes to the "recognition of the inseparability and reciprocity of form and content [which] is of course as old as Aristotle".[33] Longinus, who speaks of "Arrangement" as one of the five sources of literary excellence,[34] says that structure or arrangement does "not appear in one or two sentences; [but] must gradually become apparent as the order of the whole work is unfolded".[35] Arrangement for Longinus is composed of two parts: "One part of the process

---

[31] T. W. Baldwin, *Shakespeare's Five-Act Structure. Shakespeare's Early Plays on the Background of Renaissance Theories of Five-Act Structure from 1470* (Urbana, Illinois, University Press, 1947).

[32] René Wellek, *Concepts of Criticism*, ed. Stephen G. Nicols, Jr. (New Haven, Connecticut, Yale University Press, 1963), p. 54.

[33] *Ibid.*, p. 55. Wellek briefly traces the idea of reciprocity of form and content from Aristotle to the present.

[34] Longinus, "On Literary Excellence" in *Literary Criticism*, p. 153.

[35] *Ibid.*, p. 147.

pleases the reader by its selection of matter; the other by its
putting together of what has been chosen." [36] This Arrangement
(which is enough of a gift to warrant a man's being called an
artist even if he has not the natural gift for "excellence of expression") encompasses within its harmony of the whole, both
unity and variety.[37] Aristotle also stresses that unity of plot comes
not from its being concerned with the actions of a single man,[38]
but from arrangement:

the plot, being an imitation of an action should be concerned with one
thing and that a whole, and that the parts of the action should be so
put together that if one part is shifted or taken away the whole is
deranged and disjoined, for what makes no perceptible difference by
its presence or absence is no part of the whole.[39]

Perhaps the chief difficulty in discussions of structure is that the
uniqueness of the artistic creation is ignored. The many contradictions that Wellek sees as characterizing the many definitions
of "form" and "structure" are as numerous as the unique structures
of the work of art that underlie these critical descriptions. Rather
than turn to a preconceived notion of Aristotelian or even Shakespearean Tragedy if such concepts even exist), then, let us turn
to the specific play *Antony and Cleopatra*, and discuss its peculiar
structure, whether it be Tragedy or Roman or *sui generis*. A first
glance at the play reveals at least two things: First that the play
does not merely follow the rise-and-fall pattern of a single Aristotelian hero; and second, that it does not follow the chronological,
historical pattern of Plutarch's account. What pattern or structure
or arrangement does become clear is that of a rapid shift from
place to place and from point of view to point of view. Although
many have noted Shakespeare's technique of alternation in the
shift from Gloucester to Lear and from Egypt to Rome, few have
commented on any thematic implications of the shifting. Some
have vaguely suggested an expansiveness in keeping with the

---

[36]   *Ibid.*, p. 159.
[37]   *Ibid.*, pp. 191-193 *passim.*
[38]   See discussion above.
[39]   Aristotle, p. 81.

colossal imagery as the sole end of this shifting in *Antony and Cleopatra.*

Perhaps the best clue to the structure of the play as reflected in this rapid shift in point of view is the many contradictions of the critics after centuries of critical observation. Traversi, as we have seen, considers the dilemma in this way:

> Is *Antony and Cleopatra*, to put the matter in other terms, a tragedy of lyrical inspiration, presenting the relationship of its central figures as triumphant over adverse circumstance, or is it rather a pitiless exposure of human frailties, of dissipation of spiritual energies through wilful surrender to passion? [40]

"Both readings", Traversi assures us, "considered exclusively, depend in some measure upon a partial and incomplete reaction to the play's theme." [41] While Traversi then suggests that the only answer to his question lies in the resolution of "the interpretation of the author's intention", [42] the answer surely lies in the question itself. Rosen illuminates the questioning nature of the play when he says,

> The most important reason why *Antony and Cleopatra* has been interpreted in so many ways is that we, as audience, are constantly forced to change our point of view. At one moment we are in Egypt; suddenly we are transported to Rome. We see the actions of Antony and Cleopatra through Roman eyes and Roman judgments; we see these same actions from the Egyptian point of view; we hear the lovers' own judgments of their actions. [43]

This question structure is surely what has prompted the many critical observations of the lack of moral judgment and "ambiguity" of the play.

Although this "interrogative mood" has been noted in *Hamlet* by Maynard Mack, [44] and by Harry Levin in *The Question of*

---

[40]   Traversi, *The Roman Plays*, p. 79.

[41]   *Ibid.*

[42]   *Ibid.*

[43]   Rosen, p. 105.

[44]   Maynard Mack, "The World of Hamlet", in *Tragic Themes in Western Literature*, ed. Cleanth Brooks (New Haven, Connecticut, Yale University Press, 1960), p. 33.

Hamlet,[45] it has not been noted in many of Shakespeare's other plays. The controversy between those who would view the worlds of *Lear* as exclusively triumphant or cynical, Christian or Pagan, depends on whether the question of the justice of the gods is seen as that of Edmund or Gloucester or Kent or Lear himself. The play poses the question fully and the critics have felt a need to supply a single answer under the banner of Unity. This alternation of scenes and points of view we have already noticed in the contrasting points of view of the characters. Thus Charmian and Octavius and Cleopatra all dramatize different perspectives as clearly as do Laertes, Fortinbras, the Players, and Hamlet. While the *utile* of considering the question of the nature of love can hardly be denied, some critics seemingly would prefer the narrow dogmatism of a propagandistic "unified" answer in the drama.

Differing viewpoints concerning the question of the nature of love discussed in Chapter IV form a central question throughout the entire play. Does one merge in love or may he retain his identity? Is purely spiritual love the highest form of love? Is friendship higher than love? These are but a few of the questions of love we have seen dramatized from differing points of view in the play. The question form, moreover, characterizes many of the best considerations of the nature of love from Plato's *Symposium* on the subject to Burton's presentation of the many varied opinions of the most learned men of antiquity. Leone Ebreo presents a dialogue between Philo and Sophia in his *Diologhi d'Amore*. Castiglione in *The Courtier* remains a full and deep reservoir of information on Renaissance views of love because its many speakers present a number of points of view on the subject. As David L. Stevenson points out, "Conflicting attitudes toward love pervade" the literature of the Renaissance.[46] H. G.'s 1566 English translation of Boccaccio's *Il Filocolo* as *The Most Pleasant and Delectable Questions of Love* is but another of the works available on the questions that are no more "answered" today than in

---

45 Harry Levin, *The Question of Hamlet* (New York, Oxford University Press, 1959). Mr. Levin considers interrogation, doubt, and irony in his analysis.
46 Stevenson, p. xi.

the early seventeenth-century. The question of the nature of love, moreover, is one about which all lovers of wisdom (philosophers or not) have always thought, asked, and talked. It is a question, as we have seen, that Shakespeare is never far from considering from his earliest works onward.

The question of the nature of love appears in the play in several forms. Most, as we have seen, are dramatized; others are simply asked. Cleopatra's very first line is interrogative: "If it be love indeed, tell me how much" (I, i, 14). The line contains two questions. The first is one to which the critics have responded, "Is this indeed love, or is it lust or pleasure or *voluptas*?" [47] The second is a manifold question we have already noticed in Chapter IV. What are the limits of love? Once love reaches its "bourn", when it stops growing (and love is possessed or attained), is it any longer love? Is a divided love possible? In a structure resembling that of a dialogue or a symposium a number of possible answers to these questions are either enacted or verbally presented throughout the play.

Many of the questions of the play are merely expositional, as when Antony and Cleopatra (for most of the questions of the play are theirs) asks a messenger questions in a scene that begins *in medias res*. Other questions are more thematically provocative. Still other questions are enacted by the dramatic conflict inherent in the very juxtaposition of opposites. Many of Cleopatra's seemingly capricious questions, for example, dramatize both the conscious art of love that enables her to retain Antony, and the complete and exclusive concern for her lover. Many, indeed most, of the supposedly selfish inquiries of the Queen center upon Antony. "Where is he?" she asks Charmian (I, iii, 1). "See where he is, who's with him, what he does" (l. 3). She gives directions for Charmian according to the different moods he may be in: "If you find him sad,/ Say I am dancing; if in mirth report/ That I am sudden sick" (ll. 4-6). When Charmian proposes that she is not treating Antony as if she were in love with him, Cleopatra answers with another question, "What should I do, I do not?" (l. 8). Clearly if Charmian had offered an alternative that seemed

[47]   See discussion, Chapter IV.

more effective to Cleopatra, her concern for keeping Antony would have forced her to accept the suggestion. She is constantly wondering where he is and what he is doing: "Saw you my lord?" (I, ii, 77) "Was he not here?" She never tires of asking of him. When Mardian asks, "What's your highness' pleasure?" (I, v, 8), she replies that she takes no pleasure in anything a eunuch has. Then she asks of Antony:

> Where think'st thou he is now? Stands he, or sits he?
> Or does he walk? or is he on his horse?
>
> (ll. 19-20)

No question is trival to her when it relates to Antony. When she speaks of Antony in her mind's eye, he too is asking of her. "Where's my serpent of old Nile?" he asks (l. 25). When Alexas enters with a message from Antony, her mind is still lingering on her love: "How goes it with my brave Mark Antony?" (l. 38), she asks before he speaks. Again she is interested in his mood: "What, was he sad, or merry?" she asks. So concerned is she with Mark Antony that as audience we are as angry as Cleopatra at the response of Charmian to Cleopatra's question: "Did I, Charmian,/ Ever love Caesar so?" (ll. 66-67). When Cleopatra asks of anyone else, it is always in relation to Antony. Her questions about Octavia's height (III, iii, 11), voice (l. 12), gait (l. 17), age (l. 26), and face (l. 29) all are concerned with Octavia as her competitor. Octavia has no other existence for her – or for us.

But Cleopatra questions not only Antony's whereabouts, but the very truth and depth of the love he swears to her. From her first "if" it be love, she questions him repeatedly so that he must concern himself with the question. Indeed, we have seen that the very ritual or game of love, whereby he swears and shows his love to her, is partially accountable for the validity and depth of the love. When he swears his love for her, she prevents him from treating her like Fulvia by showing herself wise: "Why did he marry Fulvia and not love her?" (I, i, 41), she asks him. On hearing of Fulvia's death, she surprises and delights Antony and the audience by asking, "Where be the sacred vials thou should'st fill/ With sorrowful water?" (I, iii, 63). But if she questions his love, she also wonders why he should ever question hers: "Not know me yet?" she pleads (III, xiii, 157). While Cleopatra asks many questions concerning Antony, so does the mutual nature of their love dictate that he should ask many of her. He is continually concerned with her moods in his attempt to please her: "What sport to-night?" (I, i, 47); "How, my love?" (I, i, 24); "What's the matter?" (I, iii, 18); "How now, lady?" (I, iii, 39); "Where hast thou been, my heart? Dost thou hear, lady?" (III, xiii, 172); "Coldhearted toward me?" (III, xiii, 158).

As is characteristic of most of the philosophical problems that Shakespeare dramatized in his plays, the question of Antony's sovereignty is introduced early. This concern, for example, begins in the very first scene when Cleopatra challenges it (I, i, 20-32). Antony's response to her query (only one of the answers in the play) is given in his famous "Let Rome in Tiber melt" speech (ll. 33-40). The problem of Caesar's hold on Antony is reintroduced by Demetrius: "Is Caesar with Antonius priz'd so slight?" (l. 56). Indeed the debate over the relative fortunes of Caesar and Antony is a central one in the play. It is the play, not merely the Soothsayer, who must answer when Antony asks, "Whose fortunes shall rise higher, Caesar's or mine?" (II, iii, 15). Menas' repeated question to Pompey reminds us of Antony and Caesar as well: "Wilt thou be lord of all the world?" (II, vii, 61 and 62). Indeed, the symbolic level of some of the questions is seen in Agrippa's asking Enobarbus: "What's Antony?" (III, ii, 10). The play provides many answers. Is Antony merely the bellows and the fan to cool a gipsy's lust, is he the Emperor Antony, is he the brave general who ate strange flesh, is he the bounteous lord of Enobarbus? The conflict is one of those which structure the play. The critics have demanded a single answer, but the play remains provocative. "Think you there was, or might be such a man/ As this I dreamt of?" (V, ii, 93-94) asks Cleopatra. The critics, like Dolabella, have replied, "Gentle madam, no" (l. 95). Some indeed have replied with more vehemence and less decorum. But the answer is only Dolabella's and the critics', not the play's. The play centers on the question as ultimately more meaningful than any implied answer.

The many questions in the play are the issues of the play. What is Antony? "O, whither has thou led me, Egypt?" (III, xi, 51), and only a close study of the play provides the dramatic evidence for answers. "O, is't come to this?" (III, xiii, 114) asks Cleopatra and the play provides only an echoing question as its answer: "All come to this?" (IV, xii, 20). Does love have a physical basis asks the play as clearly as Mardian asks "What's your highness, pleasure?" (I, v, 8), and Cleopatra answers "I take no pleasure/ In aught an eunuch has" (ll. 9-10). Cleopatra punningly introduces the problem again in the last scene when she asks of the worm, "Remember'st thou any that have died on't?" (l. 253). The fullness of the query which the play provocatively poses surpasses even the humor of the flat statement of Rosalind that "men have died from time to time and worms have eaten them, but not for love" (*As You like It,* IV, i, 107-108). Indeed, the critics may seek, even demand, a single and absolute answer to the problem of the nature of love in *Antony and Cleopatra,* but the play remains as provocative and mysterious as the very nature of love itself. "What manner o' thing is your crocodile?" (II, vii, 40) asks Lepidus. "What colour is it of?" (l. 45), he continues, but the answers of the play are as mysterious as Antony's responses. "Will this description satisfy him?" (l. 50), Caesar asks. But the play provides only more questions and Lepidus and the critics must have as their only answer one similar to that spoken by *All* when the music of Hercules leaving Antony is heard: "Content. 'Tis strange" (IV, iv, 21). The reader and the spectator, then, may leave the study or theatre feeling intellectually provoked, rather than merely purged. It is this provocative quality of the questioning nature of many of Shakespeare's plays that qualifies them for works of art in Boccaccio's definition. *Antony and Cleopatra,* by its provocativeness, for example, "appears to be a river, if I may use the figure, both shallow and deep, in which the tiny lamb can go on its feet and the great elephant has ample room to swim." [48]

But if the enacting of a number of views concerning the nature

---

[48]   Giovanni Boccaccio, "The Life of Dante", trans. Charles G. Osgood in *Literary Criticism,* p. 208.

of love as in a dramatic symposium describes a tone and structures the play, it is surely not the description of The Structure
of the play. If the question of the nature of love is asked in the
play (and I think it is), it is also ultimately a rhetorical one. If
the first part of the play focuses on "The Everlasting No", the
second part clearly turns to "The Everlasting Yea!" And the
order (or Arrangement, as Longinus would term it) is artistic,
not accidental. As we have seen, the descriptions of "the dramatic
movement" of the play have been either of the rise-and-fall of
Antony or the rise-and-fall of Antony with another rise by Cleopatra in the Fifth Act *coda*.[49] The descriptions are Aristotelian,
rather than *Antony-and-Cleopatrian* in their orientation. The
movement of the play is from the "amusing" first part of the play
(as Bradley describes it) to the blending of the sexes (as Knight
sees it). Miss Pogson suggests the same blending of the sexes in
her assertion that the language of physical love used in the play
is analogous to the language of physical love used in religious
poetry to describe "the joy of Divine Union".[50] Miss Maizitis
notes the same universal overtones in the physical love when she
says, "For all its cosmopolitan trappings", the world of Antony
and Cleopatra "is a pastoral world, a 'new earth' where it is
possible to experience anew the myth of creation".[51] She again
notes the mythic background of the play when she speaks of the
setting of the play:

The setting in which Antony and Cleopatra exist for us retains,
despite the presence of Roman soldiers, something of the untouched
quality described in creation myths. Egypt, the very oldest of civiliza-
tions, is pictured as a sacred spot still bearing life spontaneously, as
the earth did when she was young: the very mud of the Nile breeds
strange shapes "by the operation of your sun." This is the world, in-
exhaustible and exuberant, that can afford to joke about death.[52]

If we object to the analogous structure of creation myths merely
because they seem "un-Shakespearean", we are at least in the
good company of other un-Shakespearean plays from *The Comedy*

[49]   See J. Dover Wilson above.
[50]   Pogson, p. 108.
[51]   Maizitis, p. 199.
[52]   *Ibid.*, p. 201.

of Errors to *The Tempest*. Indeed, *The Tempest* is in many ways closer to the tone and structure of *Antony and Cleopatra* than the Tragedies and Roman Plays with which *Antony and Cleopatra* is consistently grouped. Neither may we dismiss the mythic structure as the product of "modern" criticism. The patterns described by Maud Bodkin are, after all, archetypal.[53] Aristophanes speaks of the Sky Father and Earth Mother in Plato's *Symposium:*

> In the first place, the sexes were originally three in number, not two as they are now; there was man, woman, and the union of the two, having a name coresponding to this double nature. ... Now there were these three sexes, because the sun, moon, and earth are three; and the man was originally the child of the sun, the woman of the earth, and the man-woman of the moon, which is made up of sun and earth. ...[54]

Lord Gasper in *The Courtier* says (prefacing his comment with "it is the opinion of most wise men"), "Man is likened to the Forme, the woman to the Matter."[55] Surely the fullest account of the Sky Father and Earth Mother in the Renaissance is that of Leone Ebreo. Sophia in his *Dialoghi d'Amore* declares that "the marriage in love of man and woman is therefore a copy of the sacred and divine marriage of the supremely beautiful with the highest beauty, from which the whole universe takes its origin. ..."[56] Throughout the work we are reminded that Heaven as a male loves Earth as a husband does a wife.[57] Indeed, one of Shakespeare's acknowledged teachers of love, Ovid, writes of the Birth-Goddess Isis and her lover Osiris.[58] But the mythical marriage of Antony and Cleopatra as Isis and Osiris is clear in the text alone. Cleopatra's identification with Isis is her own and has often been pointed to.[59] Her association with the fertile ooze of the Nile is often made (too often to warrant its repetition here).

[53] Maud Bodkin, *Archetypal Patterns in Poetry. Psychological Studies of Imagination* (New York, Random House, 1961).
[54] Plato, pp. 50-51.
[55] Castiglione, p. 199.
[56] Leone Ebreo, p. 425.
[57] *Ibid.*, pp. 65, 82-95, 363, 368-369.
[58] Ovid, "The Loves", II, xiii, 8-18; "The Art of Love", I, 77-78 and III, 33.
[59] See, for example, Michael Lloyd, "Cleopatra as Isis", cited above.

Even a cursory perusal of the play in the mind's eye recalls Cleopatra as the serpent of the Old Nile. Knight and Charney study the images in detail for those who do not themselves recall them.[60]

The fact that it is in the day that Cleopatra dresses in "the habiliments of the goddess Isis" (III, vi, 17-18) might not be important except for the many indications that the Earth Mother is fertilized by the rain or "by the operation of your sun" (II, vii, 27) throughout the play. Emperor Antony, after all, does have "A sun and moon" in his face (V, ii, 80), and these in turn "lighted/ The little O, the earth" (ll. 80-81).[61] It is, after all, by Phoebus' amorous pinches that Cleopatra has been made black (I, v, 28; V, ii, 316). Antony addresses the sun (IV, xii, 18; cf. III, xii, 182) to which he is related as clearly as he is to Hercules, and Cleopatra addresses both the literal sun and Antony when she says immediately after he is borne dying to her, "O sun,/ Burn the great sphere thou mov'st in, darkling stand/ The varying shore o' the world" (IV, xv, 9-11). Indeed, Antony's way is consistently equated with light. Lepidus wishes him well as he says, for example, "Let all the number of the stars give light/ To thy fair way!" (III, ii, 65-66). When Antony is dying it is with an awareness that "the long day's task is done" (IV, xiv, 35) in much the same way that Iras (after his death) is aware that "the bright day is done/ And we are for the dark' (V, ii, 192-193). The clearest speech of all is Cleopatra's vision of the Emperor Antony:

> His face was as the heavens, and therein stuck
> A sun and moon, which kept their course, and lighted
> The little O, the earth.
>
> (V, ii, 79-81)

When Dolabella interrupts with "most sovereign creature", he only reminds us as do phrases like "a lass unparalleled" that Cleopatra is more than a single tragic Queen. She continues with her description of Antony:

---

[60] Knight, pp. 229-238; Charney, pp. 96-102.
[61] While earth here is undoubtedly the "o" the reference may also include the "wooden o" of the stage world as well as a sexual meaning (see Partridge).

His legs bestrid the ocean, his rear'd arm
Crested the world: his voice was propertied
As all the tuned spheres, and that to friends:
But when he meant to quail and shake the orb,
He was as rattling thunder. For his bounty,
There was no winter in't: an autumn 'twas
That grew the more by reaping: his delights
Were dolphin-like, they show'd his back above
The element they lived in: in his livery
Walk'd crowns and crownets: realms and islands were
As plates dropp'd from his pocket.

(ll. 82-92)

The lengthy speech delivered by Cleopatra in a verse heightened even for her at this climatic point in the play is hardly to be dismissed lightly. Whether the Folio reading of "Antony" or J. Dover Wilson's generally acknowledged "brilliant" emendation of "an autumn" is accepted, matters little. While "Antony" here would only add to the idea of sovereignty discussed in terms of "an Antony" (See also V, ii, 99) throughout the play,[62] the bounty of a Sky Father or some other creature of mythical stature is clear.

The progress of the play, I should like to suggest, follows the marriage of the lovers even to the birth of the baby Cleopatra sees at her breast (V, ii, 308) and to her creation of another Antony (l. 345), the Emperor Antony, who is reborn in the dream told to Dolabella. The entire movement of the play seems to imitate that of the love-act itself. While the suggestion of the structure of the play may at first seem (like descriptions of the play itself) merely gimmicky or ingenious, it hardly seems farfetched that a play about the nature of love should be so constructed. Neither Aristotle's *mimemis* nor imitation of an action need be turned to. The metaphor of the love-act as design is sustained throughout the play. The importance of this structure is seen continually from Longinus' stress on Arrangement to Kitto's assertion that "if the dramatist had something to say, and, if he was a competent artist, the presumption is that he has said it, and that we, by looking at the form which he created, can find

---

[62] See discussion, Chapter IV.

out what it is".[63] This emphasis of Kitto's, which titles his book, is clear in his statement that:

I have come to believe more firmly, and I hope to follow more consistently, as a principle of criticism, the idea that in a great work of art, whether a play, a picture, or a piece of music, the connexion between the form and the content is so vital that the two may be said to be ultimately identical.[64]

The metaphor of the love-act in *Antony and Cleopatra* is begun in the "amusing" tone of the first part of the play that Bradley sees as a blot on the purity of the tragedy. The comedy here, I have suggested,[65] functions as love play. In her attempt to avoid cloying Antony, to join with him in the humor of comradeship,[66] to remain a mystery to him after he has possessed her, to tease and to excite him are functions reflected in this comedy. She jeers and challenges his love (I, i, 14-17) and his sovereignty (ll. 18-40). The artfulness of her love and her humor (all things after all, "become her", l. 49) contrasts with the capricious folly of Charmian's love play with Alexas, the Soothsayer, and Iras (I, ii, 1-75). The comedy is but one "sport" (I, i, 47) in which Antony and Cleopatra engage. Others, of course, include fishing (II, v, 10 ff.), dancing (I, iii, 4), and merely wandering together through the streets at night (I, i, 53). Even Lepidus and Caesar speak of tippling (though Caesar derogatorily speaks so of Antony, I, iv, 19, and his "own tongue/ Splits what it speaks", II, vii, 122-123) in the first part of the play. Lepidus, of course, is so drunk that he seems "on wheels" (II, vii, 92) and misses the drunken camaraderie of the song to Bacchus (II, vi,, 111 ff.). Indeed, even the cynical commentator on Antony's levity participates in and clowns bawdily through the amusing first part of the play (I, ii, 128 ff., for example). Virtually every scene of the first two Acts is filled with love play. If Antony and Cleopatra (almost all of I, iii, for example) or Charmian and Alexas are not engaging in love play, Cleopatra is using Mardian as Antony's substitute, telling him

---

[63]   Kitto, p. v.
[64]   *Ibid.*
[65]   See discussion, Chapter III.
[66]   See discussion, Chapter IV.

playfully how "short" (II, v, 8) he comes of Antony (I, v, 7 ff. and II, v, 3 ff.). Lepidus and Antony jovially discuss the nature of love through the image of the crocodile,[67] and all is filled with images of playfulness, food, and wine. Only later in the play (III, xi) is love full of lead (l. 72), so that Antony must ask that we go to supper (IV, i, 44), scant not our cups, and be bounteous at our meals (l. 21). Ceres and Bacchus precede Venus, after all,[68] and the Egyptian food and wine in the first part of the play "ripens" toward "an Alexandrine feast" (II, vii, 95-96). Cleopatra's violence with the messenger (II, vi, 61 ff.) and Antony's with Thidias (III, xiii, 85) and the ecstatic frenzy of their death speeches are as much a part of the love-act structure as they are of the love-act.

With the background of the love play, the food, and the wine of the first two Acts, Eros is introduced by name in III, vi, 1. While this may indeed be expositional, the repetition of his name throughout the play exceeds that of any other character's. Eros' "Come, sir" (l. 24) is the last line of the scene and introduces us to the word which is used too often by him, and by Antony with him, to be accidental. In III, xi, Eros (not called here by name) pleads three times (ll. 42, 46, and 50) to Antony in the Queen's behalf, after he has (with Charmian) led Cleopatra to Antony:

> *Enter* CLEOPATRA *led* by CHARMIAN *and* EROS: IRAS
> *following.*   (SD ff. l. 24)

It is in Act IV, however, that Eros plays his most important role, for here he is as closely related to the love of Antony and Cleopatra as the relation between the man whom Antony calls, "Eros, mine armour, Eros! *Enter* EROS *with armour.*" (IV, iv, 2) and the Queen whom Antony calls "The armourer of my heart" (l. 7). The pun on *amour* is surely present here, and is repeated in IV, viii, 15. In this scene, Eros (already introduced in III, v) is called by name five times (twice each in ll. 1 and 2 and once in l. 14). The word "come" is used three times in the scene [69] – twice to

67 See discussion, Chapter IV.
68 See discussion Chapter IV.
69 See "come" in Partridge (although he gives no examples from either

Eros (ll. 3-5) and once to Cleopatra (l. 28). Indeed, Eros "fumblest" (l. 14) as clumsily as the literal and sexual death of Antony. Eros' name is again mentioned twice in scene xii (ll. 42 and 49) and fifteen times (ll. 1, 12, 18, 21, 35, 41, 62, 71, 96, 97, 101 and twice each in ll. 50 and 54) in Antony's dying (not his death) scene. The words "come" and "comes" are used eight times in the dying scene (ll. 50, 54, 63, 67, 78, 84, 126, and 137). The repetition of "come" might be denied its sexual significance but for its repetition nine times during Antony's actual death scene (IV, xv, 36, 82, 88, 90; twice in l. 29; and three times in l. 37). The fact that "welcome" envelopes the triple repetition of "comes" in l. 37 (see ll. 36 and 38) and that Cleopatra echoes the very triple use of the word in her death scene (V, ii, 47) – even adding an additional "come" in the line – only underscores its artistic deliberateness. Cleopatra also puns on the word "come" six other times in her death scene (ll. 36, 235, 286, 290, 302, 363). The word "dying" is punned on six times in Antony's death scene (ll. 7, 38 and twice each in ll. 18 and 41) and ten times in Cleopatra's (ll. 41, 45, 46, 243, 246, 248, 253, 328, 352, 354).

The language and the tone of the death scenes argues for a sexual as well as a literal death. Antony comes to death as a "bridegroom" (IV, xv, 100) and Cleopatra comes to Antony, calling him "Husband" (V, ii, 286). "Husband, I come", she declares and reminds us of Juliet's similarly sexual overtones in "Romeo, I come" (IV, iii, 58). Antony speaks of "this bloody stroke" (l. 90) that kills him,[70] and Cleopatra speaks of "What poor an instrument/ May do a noble deed!" (V, ii, 235-236). After Antony's death-stroke the second Guard declares that "the star is fallen" (IV, xiv, 106),[71] and the verb is sexually played upon by Cleopatra after Antony's actual death:

Romeo and Juliet or *Antony and Cleopatra*). For an example of a poem in which the pun is central, see Donne's "The Bridegrooms comming".

[70] Cf. *Romeo and Juliet*, V, iii, 175: "And Juliet bleeding, warm, and newly dead ...".

[71] Cf. "a starre fall" in Donne's "The Bridegrooms comming", l. 1. Cf. also discussion, Chapter V, and V, ii, 292.

> O, wither'd is the garland of the war,
> The soldier's pole is fall'n; young boys
> Are level now with men. ...
>
> (IV, xv, 64-66)

The overt sexual nature of the Clown's punning on "honesty", "lying", and the combined joy and pain of the "worm" that kills and pains not pertains more to structural than comic relief.[72] It is to Juno, the wife of Jupiter, that Cleopatra calls now (IV, xv, 34) rather than the goddess Isis. Cleopatra calls to Isis repeatedly in the first part of the play (I, ii, 61, 66, 70-71; I, v, 70; III, iii, 15, 42), but after she is led by Eros (SD ff. III, xi, 24) she never again calls to Isis, but to Juno (III, xi, 28; IV, xv, 34).

In addition to the marriage and union of the lovers in the structure of the play, there is also the suggestion of the labor of pregnancy and the subsequent birth. L. P. Wilkinson sees the suggestion of pregnancy as early as the third scene of the play, in Cleopatra's lines:

> What, says the married woman you may go?
> Would she had never given you leave to come!
>
> (ll. 20-21)

Wilkinson bases his view of Cleopatra's hint of pregnancy, not on the sexual pun in "come" here, but in his contention that "Cleopatra uses words adapted from *Heroides*, VII, 139,

> sed iubet ire deus: vellem vituisset adire,
>
> *but a god bids you go: would he had forbidden you*
> *to come,*

... and like Ovid's Dido she hints that she is pregnant".[73] The hint that Wilkinson sees is in Cleopatra's parting words to Antony (I, iii, 89-95). Indeed, the word "labour" may be punningly used to Mardian (IV, xiv, 37, 47), for the sense of pregnancy in "labour" is clear in III, vii: [74]

---

[72] See discussion, Chapter IV.
[73] L. P. Wilkinson, *Ovid Recalled* (Cambridge, University Press, 1955), pp. 413-414.
[74] The word "labour" is used in the sense of pregnancy in *Love's*

> With news the time's in labour, and throws forth,
> Each minute, some.
>
> (ll. 80-81)

This may even provide the answer to the puzzle of III, x, 10-15:

> Yon ribaudred nag of Egypt, –
> Whom leprosy o'ertake! – i' the midst o' the fight,
> When vantage like a pair of twins appear'd
> Both as the same, or rather ours the elder, —
> The breeze upon her, like a cow in June,
> Hoists sails, and flies.

The many explanations of the lines have varied from Staunton's suggestion of "tail" for "sails" to Ridley's equation of the breeze with "gadfly". Ridley compares the lines to Jonson's in *The New Inn*, V, iii, 3: "Runs like a heifer, bitten with the brieze." [75] We may find a clue to the answer in the "pair of twins", in the highly uncomplimentary image of the "ribaudred nag", and in the designated month of June. The image may be that of a pregnant or love-sick cow. If so (and I acknowledge the "if") then it is appropriately like a "doting mallard" (l. 20) that "Antony flies after her (l. 21). The suggestion of pregnancy here (and I am suggesting a symbolic birth – of their love as a child, or even a work of art as a child of the creative act; I would no more have Cleopatra enter pregnant than I would Ophelia) may also explain III, xiii, 162, when Cleopatra speaks of "the next Caesarion" after Antony has asked "Coldhearted toward me?" (l. 158). The Irving Edition glosses the line as follows: "Cleopatra appears to apply the name to Antony's offspring as an indirect compliment; as if she had said, this second Caesar's son", to which the Variorum editor adds, "Or, rather, is it not a wilful and artful oblivion that she had ever had any children of whom Anthony was not the father?" [76] Is she not here speaking of the pregnancy (either actual or symbolic) that results from her love for Antony and thus in-

---

Labour's Lost, V, ii, 521 (if not in the very title), and in *Henry VIII*, V, i, 18, 20.

[75]   III, x, 14-15n.

[76]   Both the Irving edition and Furness' own comment are cited in the Variorum edition of the play in the footnote to the line.

directly answering his question? The symbolic nature of this pregnancy is stressed even in her reported death by Mardian, when he explains "in the midst a tearing groan did break/ The name of Antony ..." (IV, xiv, 31-32). The labor of this tearing groan, of course, gives birth to her dream of the Emperor Antony just as her symbolic union with Antony as husband gives rise to the baby she dreams at her breast.

The nature of love which *Antony and Cleopatra* dramatically discusses and the love-act that structures it are as much the love of the artist for his created work as it is of the physical loving act of creation. It is the loving act of art that moves from playful infinite variety to that which shackles "accidents" and bolts up change. Cleopatra herself is reborn from

> No more but e'en a woman, and commanded
> By such poor passion as the maid that milks,
> And does the meanest chares,
>
> (IV, xv, 73-75)
> I have nothing

(after the literal death of Antony) to that woman who prepares to meet "another Antony" and can say,

> Of woman in me: now from head to foot
> I am marble-constant: now the fleeting moon
> No planet is of mine.
>
> (V, ii, 237-240)

Cleopatra is no more a physical woman under the fickle moon than Donne's lovers, whom he contrasts with

> Dull sublunary lovers love
> (Whose soule is sense) cannot admit
> Absence, because it doth remove
> Those things which elemented it.[77]

The amorous language of the death scenes of Antony and Cleopatra is repeatedly paralleled. Antony calls for wine (IV, xv, 41) and asks that he "that loves me, strike me dead" (IV, xiv, 108). Cleopatra declares, "I dare not, dear,/ Dear my lord, pardon: I dare not ..." (IV, xv, 21-22), and though she speaks of not

[77] Donne, "A Valediction: forbidding mourning", ll. 13-16.

kissing him for fear of being taken, the tone is one of feminine reluctance. The figs are mentioned twice in Cleopatra's scene (V, ii, 34, 336) and remind us of Charmian's equally sexual "I love long life better than figs" (I, ii, 32). Her constant concern now is to meet another Antony, her husband (V, ii, 27, 286, 300, 345). "The stroke of death" (like the bloody stroke that kills Antony, IV, xiv, 91) is as sexual "as a lover's pinch,/ Which hurts, and is desir'd" (V, ii, 294-295). The rebirth, the hope, the created work, of the artistic love-act is another Antony, the Emperor Antony, and the child of their love that Cleopatra sees at her breast. This child (whether viewed literally as an asp or as a work of art) is that artifact made by Antony and Cleopatra by means of a symbolic love-act.

The movement of the play, then can be described as a sustained metaphor of the love-act. The form of the play (identical with its meaning, says Kitto) follows the broad outlines of the act of love. The importance of this metaphor is not to be denied. For of all literary devices, Aristotle tells us, "much the most important is the metaphor; this alone cannot be learned from others and its use is a sign of genius, for to use metaphors well is to see resemblance".[78] For those who feel the contrived quality of the shape of the play and its excessive "modernity", I suggest a cursory glance at Puttenham's description of shaped poems,[79] or the geometric patterns of the metaphysicals. The sexual structure of a play about the nature of love is so appropriate and clear in the text of the play, that we can only add, *Se non è vero, è ben trovato.* We should be much wiser to warrant Caesar's advice in the last line of the play (instead of Johnson's view of alleged artlessness and Bradley's of the defective structure) and "see/ High order, in this great solemnity" (V, ii, 363-364).

---

[78]   Aristotle, p. 103.
[79]   Puttenham, pp. 94 ff.

VI

LOVE AND THE PLAY: TOWARDS SOME CONCLUSIONS

Although Coleridge himself observed that "great as was the genius of Shakespeare, his judgement was at least equal," [1] he labeled *Antony and Cleopatra* "wonderful" only because of its style. Others have viewed the play as a *tour de force*, "dazzling" and "spacious", but hardly "meaningful". This I-love-you-but-I-don't-understand-you approach to the play has led its critics to an infinite variety of methods in order to evade analyzing the text of the play. Attention to Plutarch's "Life of Marcus Antonius" in the translation by Sir Thomas North has more often turned us away from than guided us into the play by William Shakespeare. Elizabethan background studies of the prevailing (and single) view of Love and of Cleopatra have often been made in order to demonstrate what Shakespeare "intended" us to feel toward either. The text of *Antony and Cleopatra*, however, has remained "the most neglected" [2] and "least kindly treated" [3] of Shakespeare's major plays.

Undoubtedly the chief difficulty in understanding *Antony and Cleopatra* has been an inability to recognize its uniqueness as an artistic creation. It is not a Roman Play, "a sequel to *Julius Caesar*"; [4] it is not a pseudo-Aristotelian or Bradleyian character-tragedy. The play is far closer to *The Tempest* than to *Hamlet* or *Coriolanus*. The love of Antony and Cleopatra, then, must be judged, not by the willingly suspended personal morals of the

[1] Coleridge, II, 262.
[2] Cunningham, p. 9.
[3] Bethell, p. 116.
[4] G. B. Harrison, "Introduction to The Tragedy of *Antony and Cleopatra*" in *Shakespeare's Complete Works*, p. 1219.

critic, nor by Elizabethan attitudes, nor by the morals by which
we judge individual men and women – even royal ones. To judge
Antony and Cleopatra outside the play is to judge Jupiter or
Venus or Mars. The inconsistency of their characterizations and
the heightened level of their speeches argue for their symbolic
overtones. While Antony and Cleopatra are indeed as unique as
the "Arabian bird" (III, ii, 12) and the Royal Empress of Egypt
who is unlike all other cloying women (II, ii, 235-238), they are
also "A man who is the abstract/ That all men follow" (I, iv,
9-10) and "No more but e'en a woman" (IV, xv, 73). Cleopatra
is both "A lass" and "unparallel'd" (V, ii, 315). Their historical
existence merely enforces the validity of the symbolic roles which
they enact, for in Cleopatra's name as well as in Antony's "lay/
A moiety of the world" (V, i, 18-19). Because of their symbolic
nature, then, we should consider their existence within the context of the play (and there alone) in terms of their dramatic
sympathy and dramatic contrasts with other points of view, enacted by other characters. The audience's preference for Antony
and Cleopatra over Octavius, Charmian, Octavia, Mardian, even
Enobarbus, is the work of the deliberate artist who is thus giving
a thematic preference for the point of view of the lovers.

The bawdy, colossal, and comic speeches of the play have
often been viewed outside the context of the play itself. The
images have been catalogued and isolated. Once they have been
isolated, they have been seen as capriciously sprinkled over the
play to add to its tone. Thematic implications have been ignored.
The colossal imagery has been seen as making the play "spacious", while the comic and bawdy images have been viewed as
merely flaws. But the colossal imagery, we have seen, does more
than lend tragic Aristotelian stature to its protagonists. It dramatizes the potential sublimity of love as clearly as the comic dramatizes its ridiculousness. If Antony and Cleopatra are fools, they
have noble precedents in the foolish daring of tragic heroes from
Prometheus to Macbeth. Among the other thematic implications
of the bawdy comedy is the contrast with the coarseness of
Charmian and Iras, the dramatization of the humor of comradeship that is a part of love, and the enacting of the artistic comedy

in love that prevents cloying. The many bawdy puns and sexual images of *Antony and Cleopatra* underscore the necessary earth and water that form a basis for the fire and air of spiritual love in the play's ladder of love. The phallic qualities of the serpent and sword images need no more footnoting than the emphasis on the inadequacy of eunuchs. They ask only a careful reading in context. They ask, moreover, that the play's images be considered as they interact within the context of the entire play and accrue meanings – not that the whole play be considered as either totally holy or totally corrupt in its imagery.

The intellectual questioning of the nature of love in the play is so full that we can only wonder about those who view it solely as a kind of spacious tone poem. Among the many questions of love dramatically discussed in the play are the paradoxical search for identity and union in love, the difference between love and lust, and the limits of limitlessness of love. The play enacts many of the conflicting points of view discussed in other Renaissance considerations of the nature of love – often in the same terms. The questions of the play are as numerous as they are provocative. Is love reasonable? Is jealousy a part of love? Is a divided love possible? Is magic a part of love? What is the role of the eyes in love? Once love has been attained, how may it be maintained? Like many other Renaissance treatments of the subject, moreover, the play considers the validity of a number of points of view. Like Castiglione's symposium-consideration and Boccaccio's "most pleasant and delectable questions of love", the play dramtically considers the differing views of the philosophical question – and leaves it as that, a question. The question once stated in the play, however, by arrangement and dramatic sympathy carries within it the implied answer of a rhetorical question. We can hardly sympathize with Octavia and Octavius more than with Antony and Cleopatra.

The movement of the play also imitates the love-act. The death of Antony (as seen in the use of "Eros", "come", and "dying") followed by the death of Cleopatra and the birth of her baby (V, ii, 308-309) and the rebirth of the Emperor Antony "created" by her love are as structural as they are sexual. The water and earth of the Nile characterize Cleopatra as Earth Mother as clearly as the images of the Sun characterize Antony as Sky Father. Their marriage (V, ii, 286) is as cosmic as their relationship. The comedy of the "amusing" first half of the play (filled with humor, wine, and food) provides the love play that leads to the sexual union of the protagonists. The love-act which structures Antony and Cleopatra, moreover, is also cosmic in its inclusion of love in its broadest sense – from that of friendship to that between man and woman – even to that very act of love by which the artist "shackles accidents, and bolts up change" (V, ii, 6) in the work of art that is his created child.

The play, then, we have suggested, is not so much about intuition and reason, or the East and the West, or Love and Duty as about the nature of the many varieties of love and creation. Shakespeare surely was never very far from the subject of love from *Venus and Adonis* to *The Tempest*. It is, after all, the realm of the Poet. Indeed, Castiglione suggests, "Who applyeth the sweetnesse of musicke for other cause, but for this? Who to write in meeter, at the least in the mother tongue, but to expresse the affections caused by women?" [5] Shakespeare himself leaves us with a question about the nature of love, and we are asked to leave the theatre not purged of thought as well as emotion, but provoked to think toward some conclusions.

provokes us to think on
love

[5] Castiglione, p. 235.

BIBLIOGRAPHY OF WORKS CITED

Alighieri, Dante, *The Divine Comedy*, translated J. A. Carlyle (Temple Classics Bilingual edition) (London, J. M. Dent and Sons, 1962), 3 volumes.

Bacon, Francis, *Works*, edited James Spedding *et al.* (London, Longmans, 1870-1872), 7 volumes.

Baldwin, T. W., *The Organization and Personnel of the Shakespearean Company* (Princeton, University Press, 1927).

——, *Shakespere's Five-Act Structure. Shakespere's Early Plays on the Background of Renaissance Theories of Five-Act Structures from 1470* (Urbana, Illinois, University Press, 1947).

Bartlett, John (ed.), *A New and Complete Concordance or Verbal Index to Words, Phrases, and Passages in the Dramatic Works of Shakespeare With a Supplementary Concordance to the Poems* (New York, The Macmillan Co., 1896).

Baudelaire, Charles, *Œuvres Complètes*, edited F. F. Gautier (Paris, Nouvelle Revue Française, 1918-1931), 13 volumes.

Behrens, Ralph, "Cleopatra Exonerated", *The Shakespeare Newsletter*, IX (November, 1959), 37.

Bethell, S. L., *Shakespeare and the Popular Dramatic Tradition* (New York, Staples Press, 1944).

Boas, Frederick S., *Shakspere and His Predecessors* (New York, Charles Scribner's Sons [n.d.]).

Boccaccio, Giovanni, *The Most Pleasant and Delectable Questions of Love*, translated H. G. and put into modern English by Thomas Bell (New York, Illustrated Editions Company, 1931).

Bodkin, Maud, *Archetypal Patterns in Poetry. Psychological Studies in Imagination* (New York, Random House, 1961).

Bradley, A. C., *Oxford Lectures in Poetry* (London, Macmillan, 1934).

——, *Shakespearean Tragedy. Lectures on "Hamlet," "Othello," "King Lear," "Macbeth"* (London, Macmillan, 1905).

Brandes, Georg, *William Shakespeare. A Critical Study*, translated William Archer and Mary Morison (New York, Macmillan, 1899).

Brown, Ivor, *Shakespeare* (Garden City, New York, Doubleday, 1949).

Bryant, J. A., Jr., *Hippolyta's View. Some Christian Aspects of Shakespeare's Plays* (Lexington, Kentucky, University Press, 1961).

Burton, Robert, *The Anatomy of Melancholy*, edited Rev. A. R. Shilleto (London, G. Bell and Sons, 1903-1916), 3 volumes.

Bush, Geoffrey, *Shakespeare and the Natural Condition* (Cambridge, Massachusetts, Harvard University Press, 1956).

Butler, James D., "Platonic Allusions to Shakespeare", *Shakespeariana*, III (1886), 230-232.

——, "Shakespeare and Plato", *Shakespeariana*, II (1885), 444-446.

Campbell, Lily B., *Shakespeare's Tragic Heroes: Slaves of Passion* (New York, Barnes and Noble, 1960).

Capellanus, Andreas, *The Art of Courtly Love*, translated John Jay Parry (New York, Frederick Ungar, 1961).

Castiglione, Baldassare, *The Book of the Courtier*, translated Sir Thomas Hoby (New York, E. P. Dutton, 1956).

Cecil, Lord David, *"Antony and Cleopatra"*, The Fourth W. P. Ker Memorial Lecture delivered in the University of Glasgow, 4 May 1943 (Glasgow, Jackson, Son and Company, 1944).

Chambers, E. K., *William Shakespeare. A Study of Facts and Problems* (Oxford, Clarendon Press, 1930), 2 volumes.

Charlton, H. B., *Shakespearian Tragedy* (Cambridge, University Press, 1961).

Charney, Maurice, *Shakespeare's Roman Plays. The Function of Imagery in the Drama* (Cambridge, Massachusetts, Harvard University Press, 1961).

Clemens, Wolfgang, *The Development of Shakespeare's Imagery* (New York, Hill and Wang [n.d.]).

Coleridge, Samuel Taylor, *Shakespearean Criticism*, edited Thomas Middleton Raysor (Cambridge, Massachusetts, Harvard University Press, 1930), 2 volumes.

Craig Hardin, *An Interpretation of Shakespeare* (New York, The Dryden Press, 1948).

——, "Shakespeare's Depiction of Passions", *Philological Quarterly*, IV (October, 1925), 289-301.

Croce, Benedetto, *Ariosto, Shakespeare, and Corneille*, translated Douglas Ainslie (New York, Henry Holt and Company, 1920).

Cunningham, Dolora G., "The Characterization of Shakespeare's Cleopatra", *Shakespeare Quarterly*, VI (1955), 9-17.

Curry, Walter Clyde, *Shakespeare's Philosophical Patterns* (Baton Rouge, Louisiana, University Press, 1959).

Daiches, David, "Imagery and Meaning in *Antony and Cleopatra*", *English Studies*, XLIII (1962), 343-358.

Danby, John F., *Poets on Fortune's Hill. Studies in Sidney, Shakespeare, Beaumont and Fletcher* (London, Faber and Faber, 1952).

Donne, John, *Poems*, edited Herbert J. C. Grierson (London, Oxford University Press, 1912), 2 volumes.

Donno, Elizabeth Story, "Cleopatra Again", *Shakespeare Quarterly*, VI (1955), 227-233.

Doran, Madeleine, *Endeavors of Art: A Study of Form in Elizabethan Drama* (Madison, Wisconsin, University Press, 1954).

Dowden, Edward, *Shakspere. A Critical Study of His Mind and Art* (New York, Harper and Brothers Publishers, 1900).

Dryden, John, *Selected Dramas*, edited George R. Noyes (New York, Scott Foresman and Company, 1910).

Du Bellay, Joachim, *Œuvres Complètes* (Paris, Revue de la Renaissance, 1903-13), 4 volumes.

Ebreo, Leone (Leo Hebraeus), *The Philosophy of Love (Dialoghi d'Amore)*, translated F. Friedeberg-Sieley and Jean H. Barnes (London, The Soncino Press, 1937).

Emerson, Oliver Farrar, "Antony and Cleopatra", *Poet Lore*, II (1890), 71-77, 125-129, 188-192, 516-523.

Farnham, Willard, *Shakespeare's Tragic Frontier. The World of His Final Tragedies* (Berkeley, University of California Press, 1950).

Ficino, Marsilio, *Commentary on Plato's "Symposium"*, translated Sears Reynolds Jayne, *University of Missouri Studies*, XIX (1944), 1-247.

Gilbert, Allan H. (ed.), *Literary Criticism Plato to Dryden* (New York, American Book Company, 1940).

Granville-Barker, Harley, *Prefaces to Shakespeare* (London, Sidgwick and Jackson, 1930).

Griffiths, G. S., *"Antony and Cleopatra", Essays and Studies by Members of the English Association*, XXXI (1945), 33-67.

Grindon, Mrs. Leo [Rosa], "A Woman's Study of *Antony and Cleopatra*" (Manchester, Sherratt and Hughes, 1909).

Harbage, Alfred, *Shakespeare's Audience* (New York, Columbia University Press, 1941).

Harris, Frank, *The Women of Shakespeare* (London, Methuen, 1911).

Harrison, G. B., *Shakespeare's Tragedies* (London, Routledge and Kegan Paul, 1951).

Hazlitt, William, *Characters of Shakespeare's Plays* (London, C. H. Reynell, 1817).

Herford, C. H., *"Shakespeare's Treatment of Love and Marriage" and Other Essays* (London, Adelphi Terrace, 1921).

Horne, Herman Harrell, *Shakespeare's Philosophy of Love* (Raleigh, North Carolina, Edwards and Broughton Company, 1945).

Hubler, Edward, *The Sense of Shakespeare's Sonnets* (New York, Hill and Wang, 1952).

Jayne, Sears Reynolds, *Platonism in English Drama of the Renaissance (1442-1642)*, unpublished Ph.D. dissertation (Yale University, 1948).

Johnson, Samuel, *Lives of the English Poets*, edited George Birkbeck Hill (Oxford, Clarendon Press, 1905), 3 volumes.

——, *Works*, edited Sir John Hawkins (London, printed for J. Buckland *et al.*, 1787), 11 volumes.

Jonson, Ben, *Works*, edited C. H. Herford and Percy Simpson (Oxford, Clarendon Press, 1925-1952), 11 volumes.

Kirschbaum, Leo, *Character and Characterization in Shakespeare* (Detroit, Michigan, Wayne State University Press, 1962).

Kitto, H. D. F., *Form and Meaning in Drama: A Study of Six Greek Plays and of "Hamlet"* (New York, Barnes and Noble, 1960).

Knight, G. Wilson, *The Imperial Theme. Further Interpretations of Shakespeare's Tragedies Including the Roman Plays* (London, Oxford University Press, 1931).

Knights, L. C., "On the Tragedy of *Antony and Cleopatra*", *Scrutiny*, XVI (1949), 318-323.

Leavis, F. R., "*Antony and Cleopatra* and *All for Love*: A Critical Exercise", *Scrutiny*, V (1936-1937), 158-169.

Leet, Lenora, *Elizabethan Love Tragedy. Patterns of Love Tragedy from Marlowe to Middleton: 1587-1622*, unpublished Ph.D. dissertation (Yale University, 1959).

Leone Ebreo (Leo Hebraeus), *The Philosophy of Love (Dialoghi d'Amore)*, translated F. Friedeberg-Sieley and Jean H. Barnes (London, The Soncino Press, 1937).

Lever, J. W., "Venus and the Second Chance", *Shakespeare Survey*, XV (1962), 81-88.

Levin, Harry, *The Question of Hamlet* (New York, Oxford University Press, 1959).

Lloyd, Michael, "Cleopatra as Isis", *Shakespeare Survey*, XII (1959), 88-95.

London Times Literary Supplement, 1921.

MacCallum, M. W., *Shakespeare's Roman Plays and Their Background* (London, Macmillan, 1910).

Maizitis, Mara Ruth, *A Reading of "Troilus" and the Roman Plays*, unpublished Ph.D. dissertation (Yale University, 1959).

Marvell, Andrew, *Poems and Letters*, edited H. M. Margoliouth (Oxford, Clarendon Press, 1927), 2 volumes.

Meredith, George, *An Essay on Comedy and the Uses of the Comic Spirit*, edited Lane Cooper (Ithaca, New York, Cornell University Press, 1956).

Meres, Francis, *Palladis Tamia. Wits treasvry being the second part of Wits common wealth* (London, P. Short for Cuthbert Burbie, 1598).

Milton, John, *Paradise Lost*, edited Merritt Y. Hughes (New York, The Odyssey Press, 1935).

——, *Works*, edited Frank Allen Patterson *et al.* (New York, Columbia University Press, 1931-1938), 18 volumes.

Murry, John Middleton, *Shakespeare* (London, Jonathan Cape, 1936).

Nicoll, Allardyce, *Shakespeare: An Introduction* (New York, Oxford University Press, 1952).

Ovid, "*The Loves*", "*The Art of Beauty*", "*The Remedies for Love*", and "*The Art of Love*", translated Rolfe Humphries (Bloomington, Indiana, University Press, 1957).

Panofsky, Erwin, *Studies in Iconology. Humanistic Themes in the Art of the Renaissance* (New York, Harper and Row, 1962).

Partridge, Eric, *Shakespeare's Bawdy: A Literary and Psychological Essay and A Comprehensive Glossary* (New York, E. P. Dutton, 1960).

Pearson, Norman Holmes, "*Antony and Cleopatra*", *Shakespeare: Of An Age and For All Time*, The Yale Shakespeare Festival Lectures, edited Charles Tyler Prouty (New Haven, Connecticut, The Shoe String Press, 1954).

Peart, S. E., "The Comradeship of Antony and Cleopatra", *Poet Lore*, IV (15 April 1892), 217-221.

Plato, *The Symposium*, translated B. Jowett (Boston, Massachusetts, International Pocket Library [n.d.]),

Plutarch, *The Lives of the Noble Grecians and Romans*, translated Sir Thomas North, edited C. F. Tucker Brooke (New York, Duffield and Company, 1909), 2 volumes.

Pogson, Beryl, *In the East My Pleasure Lies. An Esoteric Interpretation of Some Plays of Shakespeare* (London, Stuart and Richardson, 1950).

Pollack, Daniel Arthur, "Again for Cydnus: An Essay on the Comic Irony of Shakespeare's *Antony and Cleopatra*", unpublished Honors Thesis (Harvard College, 1960).

Puttenham, George, *The Arte of English Poesie*, edited Gladys Doidge Willcock and Alice Walker (London, Cambridge University Press, 1936).

Ribner, Irving, *Patterns in Shakespearian Tragedy* (London, Methuen and Co., 1960).

Rosen, William, *Shakespeare and The Craft of Tragedy* (Cambridge, Massachusetts, Harvard University Press, 1960).

Schanzer, Ernest, *The Problem Plays of Shakespeare: A Study of "Julius Caesar," "Measure for Measure,"* and *"Antony and Cleopatra"* (New York, Schocken Books, 1963).

Schücking, Levin L., *Character Problems in Shakespeare's Plays* (New York, Henry Holt, 1922).

Schwartz, Elias, "The Shackling of Accidents: *Antony and Cleopatra*", *College English*, XXIII (April, 1962), 550-558.

Seaton, Ethel, "*Antony and Cleopatra* and the *Book of Revelation*", *Review of English Studies*, XXII (July, 1946), 219-224.

Shakespeare, William, *Antony and Cleopatra*, edited Mrs. Inchbald (Manchester, Longman, Hurst, Rees, and Orme [1808]).

——, *Antony and Cleopatra*, edited Maynard Mack (Baltimore, Maryland, Penguin Books, 1960).

——, *Antony and Cleopatra* (New Arden), edited M. R. Ridley (London, Methuen, 1954).

——, *Antony and Cleopatra*, edited Theodore Spencer (New York, Appleton-Century-Crofts, 1948).

——, *Antony and Cleopatra*, edited J. Dover Wilson (Cambridge, University Press, 1950).

——, *Antony and Cleopatra*, edited Louis B. Wright and Virginia A. LaMar (New York, Washington Square Press, 1961).

——, *Complete Works*, edited G. B. Harrison (New York, Harcourt, Brace and World, 1952).

——, *Complete Plays and Poems* (New Cambridge), edited William Allan Neilson and Charles Jarvis Hill (New York, The Riverside Press, 1942).

——, *The Tragedie of Anthonie and Cleopatra* (Variorum), edited H. H. Furness (Philadelphia, Pennsylvania, J. B. Lippincott, 1907).

Shaw, George Bernard, *Collected Plays* (New York, Herbert S. Stone, 1901).

Simpson, Lucie, "Shakespeare's 'Cleopatra' ", *Fortnightly Review*, CXXIX (March, 1928), 332-342.

Speaight, Robert, *Nature in Shakespearian Tragedy* (New York, Crowell-Collier, 1962).

Spencer, Hazleton, *The Art and Life of William Shakespeare* (New York, Harcourt, Brace, and Company, 1940).

Spencer, Theodore, *Shakespeare and the Nature of Man* (New York, Macmillan, 1961).

Spurgeon, Caroline, *Shakespeare's Imagery and What It Tells Us* (Boston, Massachusetts, Beacon Press, 1958).

Stempel, Daniel, "The Transmigration of the Crocodile", *Shakespeare Quarterly*, VII (1956), 59-72.

Stephen, Sir Leslie and Lee, Sir Sidney (ed.), *The Dictionary of National Biography* (Oxford, University Press, 1921-1922), 22 volumes.

Stevenson, David L., *The Love-Game Comedy* (New York, Columbia University Press, 1946).

Stirling, Brents, "Cleopatra's Scene with Seleucus: Plutarch, Daniel, and Shakespeare", *Shakespeare Quarterly*, XV (Spring, 1964), 299-311.

——, *Unity in Shakespearian Tragedy. The Interplay of Theme and Character* (New York, Columbia University Press, 1956).

Stoll, E. E., "Cleopatra", *Modern Language Review*, XXIII (1928), 145-163.

——, *Shakespeare's Young Lovers* (New York, Oxford University Press, 1937).

Stroup, Thomas B., "The Structure of *Antony and Cleopatra*", *Shakespeare Quarterly*, XV (Spring, 1964), 289-298.

Stull, Joseph, "Cleopatra's Magnanimity: The Dismissal of The Messenger", *Shakespeare Quarterly*, VII (Winter, 1956).

Suberman, Jack, *Platonism in Shakespeare*, unpublished Ph.D. dissertation (The University of North Carolina, 1955).

Swinburne, Algernon Charles, *A Study of Shakespeare* (New York, R. Worthington, 1880).

Symons, Arthur, *Studies in the Elizabethan Drama* (New York, E. P. Dutton, 1919).

Ten Brink, Bernhard, *Five Lectures on Shakespeare*, translated Julia Franklin (New York, Henry Holt, 1895).

Tilley, Morris Palmer, *A Dictionary of the Proverbs in England in the Sixteenth and Seventeenth Centuries* (Ann Arbor, Michigan, University Press, 1950).

Traversi, D. A., *An Approach to Shakespeare* (New York, Doubleday, 1956).

——, *Shakespeare: The Roman Plays* (London, Hollis and Carter, 1963).

Tuve, Rosemund, *Elizabethan and Metaphysical Imagery. Renaissance Poetic and Twentieth-Century Critics* (Chicago, University Press, 1961).

Van Doren, Mark, *Shakespeare* (Garden City, New York, Doubleday, 1939).

Vaughan, Henry, *Works*, edited L. C. Martin (Oxford, Clarendon Press, 1914), 2 volumes.

Vyvyan, John, *Shakespeare and Platonic Beauty* (London, Chatto and Windus, 1961).

Waith, Eugene M., *The Herculean Hero in Marlowe, Chapman, Shakespeare, and Dryden* (London, Chatto and Windus, 1962).

Walpole, Horace, *Letters*, edited Peter Cunningham (London, Richard Bentley and Son, 1891), 9 volumes.

Watkins, W. B. C., *Shakespeare and Spenser* (Cambridge, Massachusetts, Walker-de Berry, 1961).

Weinberg, Bernard, *A History of Literary Criticism in the Italian Renaissance* (Chicago, University Press, 1961), 2 volumes.

Wellek, René, *Concepts of Criticism*, edited Stephen G. Nicols, Jr. (New Haven, Connecticut, Yale University Press, 1963).

Westbrook, Perry D., "Horace's Influence on Shakespeare's *Antony and Cleopatra*", *PMLA*, LXII (June, 1947), 392-398.

Wilcox, John, "Love in *Antony and Cleopatra*", *Academy of Science, Arts, and Letters*, XXI (1935), 531-544.

Wilkinson, L. P., *Ovid Recalled* (Cambridge, University Press, 1955).

Wright, Austin, "Antony and Cleopatra", *Shakespeare: Lectures on Five Plays* by Members of the Department of English, Carnegie Institute of Technology (Pittsburgh, Pennsylvania, Carnegie Press, 1958).

Yates, Frances A., "Shakespeare and the Platonic Tradition", *University of Edinburgh Journal*, XII (1942-1943), 2-12.

M

I